KW-484-166

Contents

**Economics of
Public Finance**

Economics of Public Finance

L Hey BA, BSc(Econ), Dip Ed
Head of Department of Business and Administrative Studies
Tottenham Technical College

Pitman Publishing

First published 1972
Reprinted 1974

SIR ISAAC PITMAN AND SONS LTD.
Pitman House, Parker Street, Kingsway, London WC2B 5PB
P.O. Box 46038, Banda Street, Nairobi, Kenya

SIR ISAAC PITMAN (AUST) PTY. LTD.
Pitman House, 158 Bouverie Street, Carlton, Victoria 3053, Australia

PITMAN PUBLISHING CORPORATION
6 East 43rd Street, New York, N.Y. 10017, U.S.A.

SIR ISAAC PITMAN (CANADA) LTD.
495 Wellington Street West, Toronto 135, Canada

THE COPP CLARK PUBLISHING COMPANY
517 Wellington Street West, Toronto 135, Canada

ISBN *Cased Edition*: 0 273 36042 6
Paperback edition: 0 273 36043 4

G4 - B865/6:48

Printed in Great Britain
by Alden & Mowbray Ltd
at the Alden Press, Oxford

Preface

PUBLIC Finance is an interesting and important subject in its own right. It is interesting because it is continually changing its range and scope. Gone are the days when it was concerned almost solely with the tax measures of the Exchequer on behalf of the sovereign. Nowadays the public sector of the economy is of growing importance. State industries are organized on a grand scale. The effective management of the whole economy relies more and more on the use of fiscal methods. Thus the title of this book is not "Public Finance" but ECONOMICS OF PUBLIC FINANCE.

This subject is important because our lives are continuously being affected by Government action in this field. It is sensible to try to understand some of the underlying reasons for changes in Government financial policies even though there may be disagreement over the policies themselves.

It is hoped that this book will be of use to students of the subject at intermediate level. In particular, the examination requirements of the following bodies have been kept very much in mind in the writing of the book:

> Local Government Board: Diploma in Municipal Administration; Institute of Municipal Treasurers and Accountants; National Certificates and Diplomas in Business Studies and Public Administration.

Students preparing for Advanced level examinations of the General Certificate of Education may also find this work of value on certain parts of the syllabus.

I shall be grateful for any suggestions or criticisms.

L. H.

1 The Economic Framework of the Economy

THE economy may be divided into two sectors, the public and the private. The money-flows which relate to the public sector come under the general heading of public finance whilst the flows of money relating to the private sector come under the heading of private finance. Unfortunately this simple division hides the fact that the boundaries of the two sectors are often blurred and difficult to define. In which sector, for example, should we place the nationalized industries controlled by organizations known as public corporations? They would seem to be part of the public sector of the economy since they are State-owned and the members of their management boards are appointed by ministers in Parliament. On the other hand they operate in much the same way as large companies in the private sector of the economy, purchasing raw materials, employing manpower, producing an output consisting of goods or services, charging prices and making investment decisions.

THE PUBLIC SECTOR

The public sector of the economy includes not only the activities of the central Government but also those of local and regional government. These activities are not merely financial in the income and expenditure sense; they are more generally economic since they affect the utilization of resources and the distribution of wealth and income in the whole economy. Activities in the public sector impinge upon the private sector in a variety of ways. Taxation reduces the command over resources of both private individuals and business organizations. Public expenditure may have the opposite effect. For example, Government expenditure may benefit industry and trade by providing local offices where unemployed workers can register and where employers can notify vacancies. Public expenditure may

1

benefit the individual through the variety of welfare services provided.

Similarly, activities in the private sector bring responses from the public sector. Suppose the general public decide to save considerably more money than previously out of their incomes. Then there will be less spending and goods will tend to accumulate on the shelves of shopkeepers. Shopkeepers will react by cutting down orders from manufacturers who in turn respond by slowing down their production and investment plans. The level of unemployment will tend to rise and this will not only increase the work of employment exchanges but will also lead to more money being paid out in social-security benefits and less money being collected in direct taxes from individuals and companies. Thus the change in activity in the private sector will certainly be reflected in changes in public sector activities. The public and private sectors are complementary to each other and this is one sense in which our economy is a mixed economy.

What then is the proper sphere of activity of the public sector? If we look at the public sector accounts in the "Blue book" on National Income and Expenditure[1] it will be seen that the activities of the Government sector include the following:

imposing taxation and giving subsidies;
engaging in trade and production;
purchasing goods and services;
owning property and collecting rent;
issuing bonds on which interest is paid;
borrowing and lending sums of money;
making and receiving grants.

It is interesting to examine the public-sector accounts in the Blue book and reflect on the economic activities which lie behind these money flows and changes in financial assets. The public sector is extremely complex. It employs civil servants, local-government officers, teachers, technicians, police and armed forces, skilled and unskilled workers. State purchases range from pencils and paper for schools and offices to steel for rolling-stock on the nationalized railways. Though taxation is the chief source of finance for current public-sector activities a large amount of capital is raised by borrowing from the general public. The objectives of the Government sector were clearly stated by the famous eighteenth-century political economist Adam Smith in the *Wealth of Nations* published in 1776. He said that the duties of the State should consist of the provision of defence, justice and some expenditure for economic and social ends. It is this last item of Adam Smith's which has seen considerable expansion in recent times. Expenditure for social and economic ends includes such aims as the following:

---

[1]*National Income and Expenditure* (H.M.S.O.).

(a) provision of public goods and services;
(b) full employment of resources;
(c) a stable value of money;
(d) steady growth in the nation's output from year to year;
(e) a satisfactory balance of payments;
(f) a reasonably equitable distribution of income and wealth;
(g) a minimum standard of individual welfare.

A surprising fact is that some of these aims may be in conflict with each other. For example the Government may find it is difficult to achieve (b) and (c) at the same time.

Collectivism

In some countries the public sector may be so large that it completely dominates the private sector of the economy. Collectivism is the name usually given to this kind of economic system. There is a central planning authority to conduct the economic affairs of the nation. The work of the public sector in such a system may be outlined as follows:

(i) *Manpower survey*. This is one of the preliminary functions of the planning authority. A survey is made of existing amounts and kinds of available manpower and directives may be issued to training establishments indicating the likely future requirements of various types of skilled labour.

(ii) *Survey of non-human resources*. This survey catalogues the available quantities of fixed capital (e.g. land, factories, machinery) and circulating capital (e.g. raw materials, goods in process, power supplies). A plan of future investment projects is decided upon.

(iii) *Allocation of manpower and resources*. These are allotted to the various (State-owned) industries in relation to the output of goods and services which are predetermined by the planning authorities.

(iv) *Distribution plan*. The planning authority decides how the goods and services which have been produced will be distributed to the various sections of the community. This is done by adjusting wages and prices to obtain the required distribution.

Various problems are likely to arise in such a system. One such problem concerns the division of resources between current and future needs. A decision has to be made as to what resources to allocate to the production of consumption goods and services for present needs and what resources to use up in adding to the stock of capital through investment. Another problem arises when the planned totals of output are "disaggregated" into actual items of production. For example, out of an aggregate headed "clothing" a decision must be made as to the quantities of the specific items which

3

constitute the total. This decision, which will have regard to types of clothing, colours, sizes, materials, etc., may result in the over-production of some lines and the under-production of others. The element of uncertainty is present in all human affairs and no amount of careful planning can eliminate it.

Public Goods

This digression into collectivism brings out the essential nature of all economic activity whether public or private. It is concerned with means and ends. The means are the available resources both human and non-human. They include manpower, land, capital equipment, technical knowledge and enterprise. The ends are the individual and social wants which need to be satisfied. They include the elementary wants such as the desire for food, clothing, shelter and protection, as well as the more sophisticated wants such as the desire for good roads, public parks and libraries. The term "public goods" is used to indicate those goods and services which are provided by the public sector of the economy. What are the distinguishing characteristics of public goods?

In the first place it may be said that some public goods will not be paid for on a voluntary basis. In other words the user is not prepared to pay a price to cover the cost of provision. Under a system of pricing, those people who are not prepared to pay the price are excluded from enjoying the use of the good or service. This principle does not apply to some collective goods such as defence.

Secondly, this does not mean that there are no goods produced by the public sector which cannot command an economic price from individual consumers. Public goods may be divided into two categories as follows:

(i) those goods and services which satisfy needs which could have been met by private enterprise at economic prices;
(ii) those goods and services which satisfy needs which could not have been met by private enterprise.

Note that the prices charged for category (i) are not necessarily competitive prices: they may be monopoly prices or State-subsidized prices. Examples are rail services and electricity supply. In the case of the provision of water, gas and electricity (i.e. the "public utilities") it is generally agreed that a monopoly is the most efficient method of provision since considerable diseconomies would arise if these services were supplied by competing enterprises. Imagine the discomfort and unnecessary cost of laying more than one set of electricity cables in each street!

The price charged for goods and services under category (ii) is a "political" rather than an economic price. It is met out of general taxation. Examples are law and order and defence. The quantities of these goods and services are determined in a democracy through the political process of voting for parliamentary representatives who express the will of the majority. In a collectivist State the amount of provision is decided by the planning authority. In both political systems the expenditure side of the equation takes precedence and revenue is adjusted accordingly. Collective needs arise as soon as society develops. Modern communities have large collective needs. The public sector meets the cost by raising compulsory contributions in the form of taxes, in accordance with current ideas about social justice.

In the case of education and training, since this provision could possibly be met by private enterprise it might be considered to fall into category (i). In practice it falls into category (ii) since there are benefits which accrue not only to the person receiving the education and training but also to the community at large. These "neighbourhood effects" take the form of advantages to other people who benefit in many ways from living in an educated and trained community. These advantages are called "externalities" and they are characteristic of many collective goods. Of course externalities may work in the opposite direction when social costs are imposed on the neighbourhood. For example, an installation for the production of cement may deposit dust and dirt over a wide geographical area.

It is to be noted that the provision of public goods does not necessarily mean that they are produced in the public sector. A collective good such as defence is paid for out of taxation. The weapons and uniforms of the forces, however, may be produced in the private sector of the economy. In this case, an increase in the provision of this particular public good would lead to increased activity in the private sector of the economy.

THE PRIVATE SECTOR

In this sector of the economy the production of goods and services takes place in order to satisfy the wants of consumers expressed by the prices they are willing to pay. If these prices are found to be profitable the continued production of the commodity or service is assured. On the other hand, if the prices which consumers are willing to pay are insufficient to make further production worth while the commodity or service will no longer be supplied. In the private sector profitability is the motive force, operating through the price mechanism. Each purchase is a vote in favour of continued production of that commodity.

This system of competition, which was called by Adam Smith "the invisible hand guiding the economy" and to which much of

5

basic economic analysis relates, may be criticized on various counts. In certain cases the criticisms have been considered serious enough to warrant a transfer of a particular section of activity from the private to the public sector.

Consider the following examples:

1. As already mentioned, certain goods and services would not be supplied under a pricing system anyway. They are collective goods which must be provided for the community as a whole. People who do not pay towards their provision cannot be excluded from their benefits—they are there for all. Why should people make a voluntary payment towards the upkeep of the army when it is there anyway? Public goods of this nature must be paid for out of the Exchequer.

2. External economies may benefit a whole industry when they are available for all the constituent firms to share. Specialized banking and marketing institutions may develop in connection with a particular industry and these services are available to all the firms. On the other hand the operations of a business may give rise to external diseconomies for other firms in the neighbourhood. A river may become so polluted by industry that firms further downstream may have to install costly water-cleansing plant.

These social costs and benefits are not included in the private financial calculations of cost and revenue. It could happen that commercial considerations in the private sector prevented a certain project from getting started, even though there were considerable social advantages accruing from it. A choice may then have to be made as to whether the project should be started or not; and if so, whether to provide it as part of public-sector output, or whether to subsidize production in the private sector.

3. Monopolies form another basis of criticism of the private sector because they provide the opportunity for restrictive practices. These may take the form of charging different prices for the same product in different markets, taking advantage of inelastic demand conditions by contracting output and sales to obtain a high price or other forms of economic control. State policy has been directed towards the control of collective agreements in restraint of trade through the working of the Restrictive Trade Practices Acts. Large single-firm monopolies and mergers come under the purview of the Monopolies Commission. Though nationalization transferred many large organizations from the private sector to the public sector it also had the effect of creating more perfect monopolies than had existed before. Even when large monopolistic organizations continue to function in the private sector of the economy it is often the case that they are

carefully controlled and regulated by the State in the public interest. The railways in Britain provide an example of State regulation before they were nationalized.

4. A further criticism of private enterprise is that, if left to itself, the resulting distribution of income and wealth will be inequitable and, since the goods and services produced depend on effective demand (demand backed up by money) rather than on needs, there will be social injustice. It is up to the State, therefore, operating through the public sector, to aim at a more equitable distribution of income and wealth.

5. J. M. Keynes in his book entitled *The General Theory of Employment, Interest and Money*, published in 1936, drew attention to the probable causes of the "trade cycle" and pointed the way to possible remedies. Private-enterprise economies are subject to periodic booms and slumps in trade. During the depression phase of the cycle there is considerable waste of both human and non-human resources. During the boom phase, inflation produces problems of a different kind, followed eventually by the collapse of prices which accompanies the movements of the economy in the direction of the slump. Various kinds of activity in the public sector are necessary to stabilize the economy on a steady course of expansion at full employment. Action is also required from time to time to counteract regional unemployment which arises from changes in demand or in methods of production. This is one of the disadvantages of geographical and occupational specialization.

It may be said therefore that the public sector is an essential part of the economy. In the field of public finance it undertakes activities which have the following broad objectives:

(i) redistribution of income and wealth according to current views of social justice or equity;

(ii) provision of public goods through a reallocation of resources;

(iii) stabilization of the level of activity at full employment without inflation;

(iv) steady growth in national resources and in national output.

The public and private sectors are inter-dependent. Their functions in the economy are complementary. In this sense the economy is truly a mixed economy. Nevertheless there is considerable interest in the size of the public sector in relation to the rest of the economy.

GOVERNMENT POLICY

It is well to point out that public finance with its economic implications, though a major instrument of Government policy, is not the only instrument. It is often referred to as "fiscal policy" to distinguish it from "monetary policy" which is an instrument of control working through the banking system. Nevertheless these two instruments of policy are closely related and are expected to complement each other. They may be supplemented from time to time by direct controls such as the control of industrial location or of monopolistic practices. Public-sector policy usually consists of a "mix" of various kinds of instruments of control, exercised through the agency of various Government departments such as the Treasury, Department of Trade and Industry and various national, regional and local authorities. The operations of these agencies appear to be purely financial, consisting of flows of money in the form of expenditure and receipts; but underlying these monetary movements are the economic problems which give rise to them: problems of the allocation of resources, the distribution of income and wealth and full employment.

TAXABLE CAPACITY

The public and private sectors of the United Kingdom economy are roughly equal in importance. If the value of all goods and services produced in a year is taken at around £40,000 million—the gross national product (G.N.P.)—then each of the sectors accounts for a total expenditure of about £20,000 million. Taxes and social-security contributions account for approximately 40 per cent of gross national product. This leads to a consideration of "taxable capacity", or how much of the gross national product the Government can take from its citizens in taxation, etc. Whereas private individuals and firms have a given income and have to adjust their expenditure to it, this is not the case with Government. The State plans its expenditure and adjusts its revenue to meet its plans. At the same time, however, under a democracy the Government must gain sufficient support from the electorate. There must be a general feeling that the tax burden is "worth it" when compared with the benefits provided by the public sector. Under collectivism it is probable that the State would take a larger proportion in taxation than under a mixed economic system.

QUESTIONS ON CHAPTER 1

1. What do you consider to be the economic role of Government?

2. What are the aims of the State in controlling the economic resources of the nation and how is this control exercised in a mixed economy?

3. "The three main problems of private enterprise are an inequitable

distribution of income, the growth of monopoly and fluctuations in employment." How can the State contribute to the solution of these problems?

4. "Social wants cannot be satisfied through the mechanism of the price system." Discuss.

2 The Working of the Price Mechanism

In this chapter we shall consider the laws of the market and the way in which prices are determined by demand and supply.

PRICE DETERMINATION

Problems of price determination are as relevant to certain branches of public-sector production as they are to private enterprise. The managers of nationalized industries must have an eye on the market. In the light of expected demand conditions they must plan their outputs and decide on what prices to charge the consumer.

It is in the realm of private enterprise, however, under perfectly competitive conditions, that resources are allocated by the market mechanism in response to the preferences of consumers. By spending their money on the things they want most, consumers make their demands known. Producers respond because it is profitable to do so. The demand for food results in activity in retail distribution. It also stimulates production in the food-manufacturing and processing industry as well as in agriculture. In addition, the demand is felt in the capital-goods industries which produce the means of production such as agricultural machinery and food-processing plant.

DEMAND

What determines the demand for a commodity? In the first place it must be noted that the demand is made up of all the individual wants of the consumers who make up the demand side of the market. These separate wants are translated into demands as soon as they are backed up by money. It follows from this that income is one of the determinants of demand for a commodity and that changes in consumer incomes will affect the demand. A rise in incomes would be expected to react favourably on demand whilst a fall in incomes would generally be expected to react unfavourably on demand.

Price is another basic determinant of demand. One would expect that a fall in price would lead to more being demanded and a rise in price would lead to less being demanded. Consider the following diagram (Fig. 2.1):

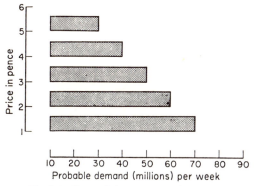

Fig. 2.1 Demand for eggs at various prices

The length of each bar represents the quantity of eggs likely to be taken off the market by purchasers each week at different prices. For example, when the price is 5p sales are likely to be 30 million per week. When the price is 2p sales are likely to be 60 million per week. Larger sales are associated with lower prices, or, to put it the other way round, at lower prices more is demanded than at higher prices. Why should this be so? The answer is to be found in the fact that at lower prices consumers will not only want to buy more but they will be able to buy more since each £ will buy more than previously. Their money will also go further if the prices of other goods on which they spend their incomes become lower than before. Thus a fall in the prices of other goods will tend to raise demand for them but will also tend to raise the demand for eggs. This follows even though eggs are relatively dearer compared with the goods whose prices have fallen. It is as though consumers had been given a rise in income. This is called the "income effect" to distinguish it from the "substitution effect" which occurs when the price of eggs falls and they are substituted for other foods because eggs are relatively cheaper and a "good buy" after their price has fallen.

SUPPLY

If we now transfer our attention from consumers of eggs to poultry-farmers and others engaged in their production we can draw a bar

11

diagram (Fig. 2.2) to show the relationship between the prices of eggs and the probable quantities which would be supplied at those prices.

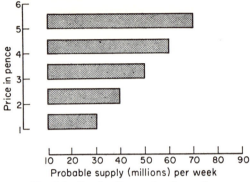

Fig. 2.2 Supply of eggs at various prices

We have used the same scales as in the last diagram. Prices are shown vertically and quantities horizontally. The length of each bar represents the quantity of eggs likely to be placed on the market each week at different prices. At a price of 5p the quantity supplied is likely to be 70 million per week. If the market price of eggs is 4p the supply is likely to be 60 million per week and so on. The bars get shorter as prices fall, indicating that smaller quantities will tend to be supplied at lower prices than at higher ones. This is a matter of profitability: if egg prices are low it will pay farmers to switch their resources to some other line of production which is relatively more profitable. Of course it may take a little time to make the necessary rearrangements but if producers believe that the low price of eggs is not just a temporary change they will gradually employ their resources in producing more profitable lines. There is another reason why more is supplied at higher prices. It has to do with the nature of short-run production. Business firms can only increase the scale of their operations in the long run. In the short run they can increase output only by making a more intensive use of their existing fixed resources such as capital equipment and buildings. When output is increased under these conditions a point will be reached beyond which the increases in output will be falling proportions of the variable inputs. This is the *law of diminishing returns* and the higher prices are necessary in order to cover the rising costs involved in producing more in the short run.

RELATIONSHIP BETWEEN DEMAND AND SUPPLY

Given the demand and supply conditions for eggs as represented in

12

the two bar diagrams, at what price is the market likely to settle down in the sense that producers are placing on the market exactly that quantity of eggs per week that consumers are willing to purchase? The answer to this question can be seen to be 3p. At this price 50 million eggs are likely to be demanded per week and 50 million are likely to be supplied per week. 3p is thus the equilibrium price which equates demand and supply. At all prices higher than 3p supply is greater than demand and the fact that producers will tend to place more on the market than consumers want to buy will exert a downward pressure on price. Similarly at all prices lower than 3p demand is greater than supply and the fact that consumers want to purchase more than is available will exert an upward pressure on price. 3p is the only price which brings the market into equilibrium.

This can be shown on a diagram which is much used in economics. This shows the supply and demand curves on the same scale (Fig. 2.3).

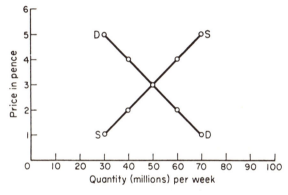

Fig. 2.3   Supply and demand curves for eggs

The demand curve (*D*) is drawn by joining the dots which represent the ends of the bars in Fig. 2.1. The supply curve (*S*) is similarly obtained from Fig. 2.2 by joining the dots which represent the ends of the bars. The equilibrium price of 3p can be read off where the two curves intersect as also can the equilibrium quantity of 50 million per week. The downward-sloping demand curve illustrates the fact that at lower prices more will be bought, whilst the upward-sloping supply curve indicates that at higher prices more will be produced. The equilibrium price is the only price which equates supply and demand.

A distinction must be made between a movement along the demand or supply curve in response to a price change and a movement of the actual curve. This distinction can be illustrated with reference to

13

the demand curve and the effect of an increase in the incomes of consumers. A shift in the supply situation may be illustrated by the effect of a tax on producers. Consider first the effect on demand of an increase in incomes. This will mean that consumers will have more money to spend on the commodity and that the amounts demanded at each price will increase. In Fig. 2.4 the supply curve is S, the old demand curve is D and the new demand curve resulting from an increase in consumer income is N. The diagram shows that an increase in demand tends to raise the price and extend the supply (along the supply curve).

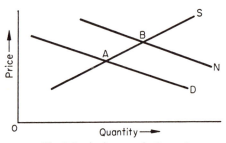

Fig. 2.4   An increase in demand

The equilibrium price and quantity has moved from A to B. Similarly a decrease in demand would tend to lower the price and reduce the quantity sold (along the supply curve). New demand curves are necessary whenever changes in income or changes in preferences occur.

A parallel analysis can be applied to the case of a change in supply. If the Government imposes a tax on the producers of a commodity with an effect similar to an increase in raw-material costs the result will be to shift the supply curve to the left since the suppliers will require a higher price to produce the same quantity as before, or, in other words, they will supply less at each price because of the tax. Fig. 2.5 shows the demand curve (D), the old supply curve (S) and the new supply curve (N) resulting from the tax.

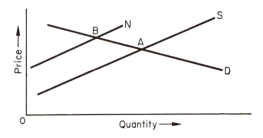

Fig. 2.5   A decrease in supply

The decrease in supply tends to raise the price and reduce the quantity sold (along the demand curve). The equilibrium price and quantity has moved from *A* to *B*. Similarly an increase in supply will tend to lower the price and extend the quantity sold (along the demand curve).

The principles of supply and demand may be listed as follows:

1. A larger quantity will be demanded at lower prices and a smaller quantity at higher prices.

2. A larger quantity will be supplied at higher prices and a smaller quantity at lower prices.

3. The equilibrium price equates the quantity supplied with the quantity demanded.

4. An increase in demand will raise the price and extend the supply; but if there is a decrease in demand the price will fall and the supply contract.

5. An increase in supply will lower the price and extend the demand; but if there is a decrease in supply the price will rise and the demand contract.

Note the difference in meaning between an extension of demand or supply and an increase in demand or supply. There is a similar distinction between a contraction of demand or supply and a decrease in demand or supply.

Having listed these principles it must be said that not all commodities exhibit these relationships. There are exceptions, some of which may be mentioned.

First, commodities may be found which do not obey the rule that less will be demanded at higher prices. Such is the case with things like bread, rice or potatoes in countries where, for the majority of people, these goods form a high proportion of their expenditure. At higher prices more may be demanded, since these are still the cheapest foods that can be obtained in the quantities required and the consumption of higher-priced foods such as meat may be reduced. Commodities which respond in this way to price changes are known as "inferior goods".

Another example is when goods of a high price are bought in preference to those of a low price because price is thought to indicate quality. Other goods act as "status symbols" (diamonds, for example) and a fall in price may result in less being demanded.

Secondly there may be exceptions to the rule that more will be supplied at higher prices. It may happen that the supply of something is completely fixed in amount and cannot be increased. Such is the case with land in the centre of a city. A famous painting such as the "Mona Lisa" is in completely fixed supply. It is said that the supply curve of labour is backward-sloping, indicating that above a certain earnings rate more leisure is preferred to more income.

Elasticity

The responsiveness of demand and supply to small changes in price may be estimated by working out the price elasticities. These are found by comparing the changes in quantities demanded or supplied with the change in price giving rise to them. All the changes are measured proportionally. Consider the following example:

Price (p)	Quantity demanded (q)	Revenue (p × q)
10	5,000	50,000
9	6,000	54,000
8	7,000	56,000
7	8,000	56,000
6	9,000	54,000

The first two columns (price and quantity) form what is known as a demand schedule. The third column shows that revenue increases at first and then falls off as prices become lower. The response of demand to a fall in price from 10p to 9p can be found by calculating the elasticity of demand. This is the proportional change in demand divided by the proportional change in price which gave rise to it. When price falls from 10p to 9p the change in price is 1p and the proportional change in price is $\frac{1}{10}$. The change in quantity demanded is 1,000 and the proportional change in quantity is $\frac{1,000}{5,000}$ or $\frac{1}{5}$.

Thus the elasticity is $\frac{1}{5}$ divided by $\frac{1}{10}$
which is the same as $\frac{1}{5} \times \frac{10}{1}$
i.e. an elasticity of 2.

When price falls from 7p to 6p, elasticity is given by

$\frac{1}{8}$ divided by $\frac{1}{7}$ ˎ
i.e. an elasticity of 0·875.

If elasticity is greater than 1 (as it is between 10p and 9p) the reduction in price will increase sales more than in proportion and total revenue will rise. On the other hand, if elasticity is less than 1 total revenue will fall (as it does between 7p and 6p). When elasticity of demand is exactly equal to 1, revenue remains the same. An elastic demand is one which has an elasticity greater than 1. An inelastic demand is one which has an elasticity of less than 1. If the elasticity is exactly 1, the demand is said to have unitary elasticity. Most demand curves are probably elastic over one part of their range and inelastic over another part. The more substitutes there are for a commodity, the more elastic its demand is likely to be in response to price changes. Although a commodity such as salt may be said

16

to have an inelastic demand, if there are several different brands on the market the demand for any one brand is likely to be fairly elastic.

It may also be the case that at high prices the demand for a commodity is elastic, but at low prices inelastic. A fall in price from 50p to 49p requires only a two per cent increase in demand to maintain total revenue; but a fall in price from 10p to 9p requires a ten per cent increase and this may be unlikely to happen.

The demand for a commodity not only responds to changes in its own price but is also affected by changes in the prices of other goods and by changes in incomes. The response of demand to a change in incomes is known as the "income elasticity of demand". The response of demand to changes in the prices of other goods depends on whether they are complementary goods or substitutes. If they are unrelated goods the response will be negligible.

A fall in the price of substitutes would tend to reduce the demand for a commodity and a rise in the price of substitutes would tend to increase it. In the case of complementary goods, however, the effect on the demand for a commodity of a change in the price of a complementary good would depend on its relative importance in the consumers' expenditure pattern. There is a "joint demand" for shoes and shoelaces but a change in the price of the latter is not likely to affect the demand for shoes. Electricity is a complementary commodity to electric heaters and, in this case, a change in the price of electricity may well affect the demand for heaters.

The elasticity of supply refers to the response of supply to a small change in price. The proportional change in supply is first calculated. This is divided by the proportional change in price which gave rise to it. Consider the following supply schedule:

Price (p)	Quantity supplied (q)
6	4,000
7	6,000
8	7,000
9	8,000
10	8,500

The response of supply to a rise in price from 6p to 7p can be found by making the following calculation:

The proportional change in supply is $\frac{2,000}{4,000}$ or $\frac{1}{2}$
The proportional change in price is $\frac{1}{6}$
The elasticity of supply is $\frac{1}{2}$ divided by $\frac{1}{6}$ or 3.

Supply may be elastic or inelastic, at a particular price, and at a particular point in time. An industry may be unable to meet an increase in demand until more factories have been built and equipped. In this case we say that supply is inelastic in the short run but elastic in the long run. The increase in demand will tend to raise the price fairly steeply, but when the industry has had time to increase its scale of operations the price will probably fall again. The increases in output which result from increasing all the inputs or factors of production, fixed as well as variable, are known as returns to scale. If there are increasing returns to scale, long-run costs will be falling; if there are decreasing returns to scale, long-run costs will be rising; and if returns are constant, so also will be costs. The costs in question are the average costs (and the marginal costs).

COMPETITION, PARTIAL COMPETITION AND MONOPOLY

When consumers have only one source of supply for the satisfaction of a particular want they are in a weak bargaining position. In this case monopoly is said to exist. On the other hand, when there are many alternative sources of supply and consumers are knowledgeable about prices and qualities available, competition is said to exist. If the number of independent producers of a commodity is substantially reduced, competition will be only partial, and if this trend continues a monopoly may be the result.

The competitive process is continually introducing change into the market situation through new products which take the place of existing ones, through lower prices for existing products and through advertising in order to stimulate sales. Many business firms operate in partially competitive conditions since they are able to change their prices or vary their products in order to increase their sales. Advertising and making a firm's product look different from that of its competitors will generally increase that firm's share of the market. In the case of monopoly a firm has captured the whole market and there are no immediate competitors. Once a monopoly has been established it may be difficult to alter the situation since the technical process may be so expensive in terms of capital equipment that there is a financial barrier to the entry of new firms. Monopolies also arise when producers make agreements between themselves in order to eliminate competition.

1. Competition

In the case of a large number of producers and consumers with knowledge of available prices and qualities and with no barriers to mobility, competition may be almost perfect in the sense that the price determined by the market and no supplier has any control over the price. Each firm is producing an identical product and aims to obtain maximum profitability from its operations. The market price is taken into account by each business and each additional unit of sales will add to the firm's revenue an amount of money equal to the price. This is illustrated in Fig. 2.6 where price is determined by the intersection of the market supply and demand curves and this price is taken as an economic fact by the business firm, as shown on the right-hand diagram.

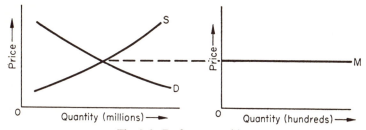

Fig. 2.6   Perfect competition

It is also taken as an economic fact by all the other firms in the industry. Whereas the demand for this particular commodity has an elasticity which probably varies along the market-demand curve, the sales curve of the individual business is perfectly elastic under these conditions.

S and *D* are the supply and demand curves relating to an industry composed of a large number of firms. *M* is the sales curve of any one of these firms. It indicates that each firm decides on what quantity to produce and market in the light of the given price. Note the different scales along the horizontal axes.

2. Partial Competition

This may take various forms but the most usual are monopolistic competition and oligopoly. In the former case there are many competing producers but each producer has managed to gain some control over the price of his product by making it different in some way from the products of other firms. This is known as product differentiation. Oligopoly occurs when there is only a small number of firms in competition with each other. Under partial competition firms are able to raise their prices a little and still retain a share of the market. This would be impossible if competition were perfect. Also under partial competition a firm may gain a few customers from its competitors by lowering its price a little. Thus, under these conditions, the sales curve of each individual firm is not perfectly horizontal but slopes downwards indicating that a lower price will result in some additional sales. In this case it is not the price which has to be taken into account by each business, when deciding whether to try to increase its share of the market, but the marginal revenue, i.e. the revenue from selling one more unit of output.

19

An example will make this clear:

Sales	Price	Revenue	Marginal Revenue
	p	p	p
100	20	2,000	—
200	15	3,000	10
300	10	3,000	—

When sales increase from 100 to 200 as a result of a price reduction from 20p to 15p, revenue increases from 2,000p to 3,000p. This is a revenue increase of 1,000p and a sales increase of 100. Thus, each sale has increased revenue by 10p. When sales increase from 200 to 300 on reducing the price to 10p there is no increase in revenue; it remains the same at 3,000p. Hence there is nil marginal revenue.

It is the marginal revenue that the manager of a business must take into account when assessing the profitability of increasing the firm's output in order to gain a larger share of the market. On the other hand, it is price, and not marginal revenue, which is taken into consideration by consumers when deciding how much to purchase. Note that the marginal revenue is less than the price when the latter is falling.

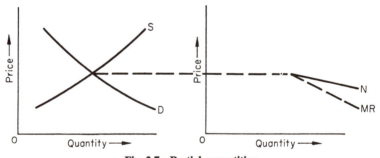

Fig. 2.7 **Partial competition**

In Fig. 2.7 market price is assumed to be determined by the supply and demand curves on the left-hand diagram. The firm (represented by the right-hand diagram) accepts the market price but finds that by making its product different from those of other producers it can extend its market appreciably by lowering price. This firm's sales curve is *N* but it must now take account of the extra revenue gained from each addition to output and sales. *MR* is the marginal revenue and is less than price.

In the case of oligopoly, a business which lowers its price will probably induce the other firms to lower theirs. If it raises its price the probability is that the others will leave theirs as they were. Thus the sales curve is likely to be inelastic at prices above the ruling price and elastic at prices below it. There may be a good case for letting things stay as they are, and using an advertising campaign to attract a larger share of the market.

3. Monopoly

Since the monopolist is the only producer in the market he can fix his price, as he has no competitors to consider. On the other hand, the monopolist's sales curve is exactly the same as the market-demand curve and therefore he must lower his price in order to increase sales. This means that marginal revenue is the important factor to consider from the viewpoint of profitability. Marginal revenue will be less than price at each quantity sold. It can be argued that monopoly output will be less than the output which would occur under competitive conditions, but this depends on the underlying conditions of production of the monopolist. He may be in a position to make full use of increasing returns to scale. A change in demand conditions in an industry may leave competitive firms with a temporary surplus capacity. Thus a programme of rationalization may be required in order to remove the surplus capacity. This would mean reorganization into larger units, aided possibly by some official body.

In the United Kingdom monopoly has been investigated by the Monopolies Commission which has been concerned mainly with single-firm monopolies and mergers. Monopolistic agreements, of the cartel type, between a number of firms, have been subjected to the Restrictive Trade Practices Act under which agreements are registered and may be examined by a Restrictive Practices Court. It is up to the firms who have made the agreement to show that it is in the public interest.

APPLICATIONS OF SUPPLY AND DEMAND ANALYSIS

(i) The Effect of a Tax on a Commodity

In Fig. 2.8 (see page 22) let D and S be the demand and supply curves for a commodity produced under competitive conditions. If a tax is imposed on the suppliers there will be a decrease in supply and the new supply curve is represented by T. Since each quantity supplied must now bear the tax this is represented by the vertical distance of the new supply curve above the old one. In other words the tax is shown by AC. The price does not rise by the full amount of the tax, however. This can be seen by comparing the broken lines AB and AC. The price has risen by an amount equal to AB to give a new equilibrium of demand and supply at A. The tax per unit of output is represented by AC which is greater than AB. The fact that sales have fallen at the new equilibrium means that the

21

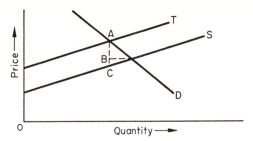

Fig. 2.8   Imposition of a tax on a commodity

tax is borne partly by the producers and partly by the consumers. Just what proportion is borne by each group depends on the elasticities of demand and supply. If supply were completely inelastic in the sense that producers placed their output on the market each day and accepted whatever price they could get for it then they would bear the full amount of the tax. On the other hand if demand were completely inelastic in the sense that consumers were prepared to take a fixed amount each day, no matter what the price, then they would bear the full amount of the tax. In practice the result is likely to lie somewhere between these two extremes.

(ii) Fluctuations in Agricultural Prices

Whereas with manufacturing industry a change in demand will generally result in a gradual adjustment of supply, in agriculture the conditions of production are such that there is usually a time lag between seed-time and harvest. This can be illustrated on the supply/demand diagram (Fig. 2.9) by assuming that the demand curve relates current demand to the market price, but the supply curve

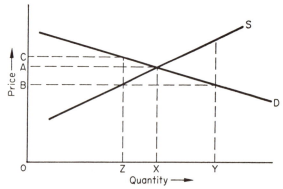

Fig. 2.9   Fluctuations in agricultural prices

relates the supply that will be forthcoming after the time lag, to market price. It can be seen from the diagram that the equilibrium price is OA and quantity OX.

This equilibrium may easily be upset, however, if for some reason actual output does not fulfil expectations. Suppose that in the next year there is an exceptionally good harvest which results in an amount OY being supplied. In order to clear the market, price must fall to OB which farmers regard as too low. They will therefore contract their supply (after the time lag) to OZ. Consumers, however, will be willing to pay OC for this amount, so price rises again.

Whether this fluctuation in prices will tend towards an equilibrium position or not will depend on the elasticity of demand and supply as well as on the vagaries of the weather. The State may decide to assist farmers to overcome this problem by subsidizing them in some way. One such method is the use of "deficiency payments". "Guaranteed prices" are agreed with the farmers through their union and if the market price is less than the guaranteed price for that particular commodity the deficiency is made up by the Government from the Exchequer. On the other hand, if the market price rises above the guaranteed price there is a gain to the Exchequer. One of the problems associated with this method of assisting agriculture is that there may be a tendency to over-produce since producers get the guaranteed price for the whole of their output. Thus it is necessary to use a quota system in order to limit production.

Alternative ways of assisting farmers include crop-restriction agreements by which, in return for a money payment, the supply of a commodity is restricted in order to secure a higher price; and crop-purchase agreements by which the Government purchases part of the supply so that farmers receive a price which is higher than the equilibrium price. The more inelastic the demand for the commodity in question the more successful these policies are likely to be in raising the price.

(iii) A Subsidy to Encourage Production

Suppose that a subsidy is given to the producers of a commodity in a competitive industry. In Fig. 2.10 S and D are the supply and demand curves, OP and OQ the equilibrium price and quantity before the subsidy. In order to encourage an output of OX a subsidy of so much money per unit of output is given. This subsidy is represented by TW. It will encourage the production of output OX since the producers will receive a price of XT and consumers will pay a price of XW. Notice that the price OP has not fallen by the full amount of the subsidy but only by MW. The subsidy is shared by producers and consumers depending on the relative demand and supply elasticities.

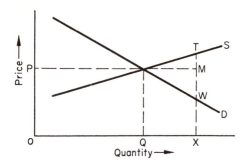

Fig. 2.10   Subsidy to producers

QUESTIONS ON CHAPTER 2

1. For what reasons may it be necessary for the Government to interfere with the free working of the price mechanism?

2. Consider the following conditions:
   (*a*) elastic demand;
   (*b*) elastic supply;
   (*c*) inelastic demand;
   (*d*) inelastic supply;
   (*e*) completely inelastic supply.
   (i) Which of the demand conditions (*a*) or (*c*) would be likely to secure the greater revenue from the imposition of a tax on a commodity?
   (ii) Which of the supply conditions (*b*), (*d*) or (*e*) would be likely to be applicable to the supply of land in the centre of a city and how would the price of such land be affected by these conditions?
   (iii) "An increase in demand will tend to raise the price and extend the quantity supplied." Illustrate this statement under conditions (*b*) and (*c*) using a supply and demand diagram.
   (iv) Show on a supply and demand diagram how a maximum price, imposed by law, would affect the price/output relationships of a commodity under conditions (*a*) and (*c*).

3 The Economics of the Production Process

In the last chapter we learned about the laws of the market and how prices are determined by demand and supply. In the present chapter we shall examine the economics of the production process paying particular attention to the cost incurred in producing an output. This cost may then be compared with the revenue from selling the output on the market. The difference between the two is profit or loss depending on whether the total sales revenue is greater or less than the total production cost.

In the production process, where an output of goods is being produced from a set of inputs, there is a relationship between inputs, costs, output and revenue which is of crucial importance to management. This is so whether the enterprise is in public or private ownership.

OPTIMUM USE OF RESOURCES

A primary reason for studying the relationship between inputs and output is to estimate the cost of utilizing resources in adding to the output of one commodity rather than another. The "opportunity cost" of increasing the output of coal by another thousand tons is the additional steel which could have been produced with the resources used for coal. In order to ensure an optimum use of resources there should be some way of comparing the benefits of the additional steel with the benefits of the additional coal. We are here concerned with marginal additions to, or subtractions from, large total outputs.

Later in this chapter it will be shown that under extremely competitive market conditions the marginal cost of each firm's output tends to equal the price consumers are willing to pay for that output. Resources tend to be efficiently allocated under these conditions since the value of marginal inputs of resources equals the value of marginal outputs. Unfortunately, this optimum allocation of resources may be upset in practice, for the following reasons:

1. The distribution of income and wealth may be regarded as in need of adjustment on equity grounds.
2. The prevalence of monopoly and other forms of market imperfection may result in prices being higher than marginal costs.
3. A divergence between private costs and benefits and social costs and benefits may result from "externalities" of one kind or another.

There are various conditions under which production may occur. Four of these will be mentioned:

(i) a small business operating under competitive conditions in a large market;
(ii) a large business operating under monopoly conditions in a large market;
(iii) a firm which is operating under partially competitive conditions somewhere between (i) and (ii);
(iv) a public enterprise or nationalized industry operating under conditions similar to (ii).

There are many variants of these but monopoly elements are absent only in (i) and it is only under competitive conditions that resources are efficiently allocated through the market mechanism. Even so, social costs and benefits may be important although they are not taken into account.

How can we measure the benefits and costs of producing more steel rather than additional coal? Looking at the benefits side it may be said that the immediate benefit to consumers can be measured by the values placed by them on extra units of coal and steel; in other words, by the price consumers are willing to pay as shown in the demand schedule. As more of these goods are produced they become relatively less scarce and their values to consumers (i.e. their prices) will fall in relation to the prices of other goods.

There may, however, be other benefits to which a value can be assigned. For example, there may be social benefits in the form of a reduction in the level of unemployment as unemployed miners or steelworkers are taken into the labour force. Thus social-security payments will be reduced. Other social benefits may accrue to other sections of the economy and it may be possible to place a value on them. On the cost side it is not only the extra cost incurred in the production of the additional coal or steel which must be considered but also such social costs as the pollution of the air and rivers, road or rail congestion, etc.

Having valued the marginal benefits and marginal costs in the case of steel and coal, then in either case welfare could be increased where these values diverged. If the benefits from extra steel were valued more highly than the costs, welfare could be increased by expanding output to the point where they were equal. If the costs were higher than the benefits, a reduction in output would be indicated. Applying this principle generally, optimum output would occur when all products were being produced in those quantities which balanced their costs and benefits, looking at each product individually. Commercially speaking, the benefit of a product is reflected in the price paid for the last unit of output produced. The cost is the financial cost of producing the last unit. Thus, marginal cost equals price. This is the case under competitive market conditions where an industry consists of many business firms each producing a more or less identical product. Under these conditions it may be relatively easy to distinguish commercial costs and benefits from social costs and benefits. When we are discussing a monopoly, however, whether private or public, it may not be easy to disentangle the purely commercial costs and benefits from the social ones.

Looking at monopoly purely from the commercial angle, it is noticeable that the price at which the product can be sold is not simply market-determined. The business itself is in a position of influencing the price in the sense that management may decide on a price to see how much output they can sell; or they may reduce output somewhat in order to obtain a higher price for less production. What is relevant both to the private monopoly and the State monopoly is marginal revenue rather than price. If 100 articles are being sold at £1·25 each and in order to sell 120 the enterprise must accept a price of £1 each, it will obviously not be worth it.

INPUTS, OUTPUT AND COST

Whenever anything is produced costs are incurred in its production. This is so whether we are speaking about private enterprise or nationalized industry. Certain costs are fixed and do not vary as output is increased or decreased. Other costs do vary with output and are therefore called variable costs. We can use the same analysis for private and public enterprise provided we understand that by doing so we are judging both kinds of enterprise by the commercial criterion of profitability or the ability to earn a surplus over cost of output. Although it may seem that the commercial criterion is the natural one to use, it must be stated immediately that it may not be the appropriate one. Performance may be judged according to a wider economic criterion which includes social costs in addition to those affecting the user; and which includes the valuation of social benefits as well. An even wider socio-political criterion may be employed in order to bring into consideration such factors as equity, political expediency, etc. These criteria may be applied to both private and public enterprise. Nevertheless, in what follows we shall concentrate on the commercial aspect of profitability.

Consider Fig. 3.1, which indicates the nature of the production process and the generation of cost:

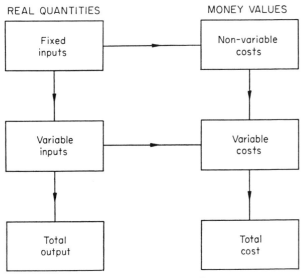

Fig. 3.1 Inputs, output and costs

The total output produced in the process of production will vary in size according to the way the variable inputs are changed. In the diagram we are assuming that certain inputs are fixed in quantity and cannot be increased or decreased in the time over which we conduct our inquiry. We are concerned with performance in the short run during which certain factors of production cannot be varied. These are represented by the top rectangles and include such items as factory or workshop complex, administrative buildings, staff salaries (in so far as these cannot be varied), local rates, depreciation charges, payments of interest to bondholders, etc.

In the next rectangle (below) the variable inputs are represented. These include quantities of raw materials, more of which will be required if output is to be increased; less of which will be required if output is to be decreased. Other inputs falling into this category are power supplies, certain types of labour, wrapping materials, etc. The costs to which these inputs give rise are variable costs. In contrast, fixed inputs give rise to non-variable costs which remain the same in the short run whether output is being stepped up or slowed down. From the diagram it can be seen that these two kinds of cost together make up the total cost of the whole output produced.

Once an enterprise is established there is generally a good case for expanding output. The greater the proportion of fixed inputs the greater the case since non-variable costs will be spread over a larger and larger output. This will lead to a gradual reduction in average cost which is found by dividing the total cost by the total output. Consider how the average cost of motor-cars can be reduced as output is expanded. Consider how the average cost of coal may vary as output is increased. In the case of coal it may very well be that average cost will rise. This draws attention to the fact that not all industries are "decreasing-cost industries". It also calls attention to the fact that "decreasing returns" may set in after a certain point has been reached in the process of expanding output. The principle of decreasing returns means that, as we continue to increase output by utilizing more variable inputs (raw materials and labour) with our fixed inputs (plant and equipment), the proportional additions to output will diminish (relative to the proportional increase in the variable input). In other words we are making the fixed inputs more and more scarce and we are getting further and further away from the most efficient combination of variable and fixed inputs. Average cost will rise as a result and the rise will become more and more

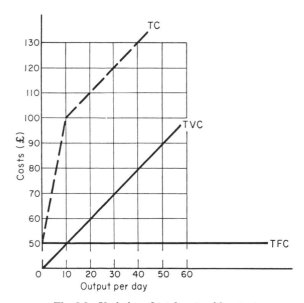

Fig. 3.2 **Variation of total costs with output**

steep as the process continues. What has happened is that the principle of diminishing returns has begun to outweigh the spread of overheads. Although average costs were falling, at first, as output was increased, they are now rising.

In Fig. 3.2 costs are measured vertically and output horizontally. *TFC* is total fixed cost. This cost stays at £50 as output changes from nil to 40 per day. *TVC* is total variable cost. It rises from nil when there is nil output to £80 when there is an output of 40 per day. The broken line *TC* shows that total costs are made up of *TFC* and *TVC*. When output is nil, *TC* is £50 and when output is 40 per day, *TC* is £130. Although these relationships have been drawn as straight lines for convenience, in practice the *TVC* and *TC* lines will tend to rise more steeply as an output of 40 per day is approached. This would reflect the increasing importance of the principle of diminishing returns as the fixed inputs were made relatively more scarce leading to smaller and smaller proportionate increases in output.

If we now divide each level of cost by the output which has given rise to it, we obtain a series of average costs as follows:

Output per day	Average fixed cost	Average variable cost	Average total cost
0	∞	0	∞
10	5	5	10
20	$2\frac{1}{2}$	3	$5\frac{1}{2}$
30	$1\frac{2}{3}$	$2\frac{1}{3}$	4
40	$1\frac{1}{4}$	2	$3\frac{1}{4}$

The symbol ∞ means that the cost is infinitely high.

The figures may be obtained from Fig. 3.2 by dividing *TFC*, *TVC* and *TC* by the relevant output.

These average costs may be shown on a cost diagram as in Fig. 3.3 (the first row of figures has been left out for convenience, otherwise a much larger graph would be needed).

In the diagram (Fig. 3.3) *AFC* shows average fixed costs, *AVC* shows average variable costs and *AC* shows average total costs. Note that as output increases these average costs are falling. Note also that they are falling less and less rapidly as output is increased. In fact it is usual for the average cost and average-variable cost to reach a minimum point and start rising again as output is expanded. This happens in the short run when the force of diminishing returns is so strong that it outweighs the effect of spreading the fixed costs. Thus the *AC* curve will be "U" shaped as in Fig. 3.4.

If they look ahead a number of years the management may find it possible to reduce costs by altering methods of production resulting in greater or smaller fixed costs. In this case a new *AC* curve will have to be drawn to reflect the new conditions. If we assume that

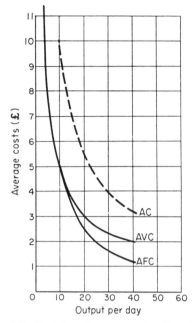

Fig. 3.3   Variation of average costs with output

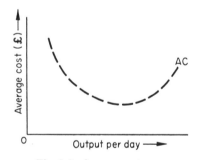

Fig. 3.4   Average-cost curve

management will try to produce at minimum average cost, the long-run cost curves will be found by joining the minimum points of the short-run curves. In present circumstances, however, it is the short-run position which is important. As long as there is sufficient revenue, from sales of output, to cover total costs, we can say that the enterprise is commercially sound. The normal profit for the industry is included in the average cost. In other words (assuming all output is sold)

$$\text{Sales} \times \text{Price} = \text{Output} \times \text{Average cost}$$

31

This would apply to a State enterprise as well as to private enterprise. In the case of the State enterprise normal profit would be replaced by normal surplus.

The left-hand side of the equation can be shown on our previous diagram if we assume the price is OP and the output/sales OX. This is shown in Fig. 3.5 as follows:

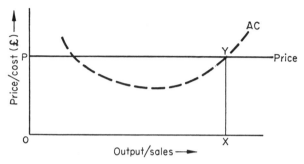

Fig. 3.5   Total revenue equal to total cost

In this diagram sales × price is represented by $OX \times XY$ and output × average cost is represented by $OX \times XY$, so that these two sums of money are equal. In other words, total revenue equals total cost, and management is breaking even and just earning the normal profit for the industry.

In the case of a State-owned enterprise, since there are no shareholders to whom dividends are distributed it is usual to use the terms "surplus" and "deficit" rather than "profit" and "loss".

MARGINAL COSTS AND PRICE

An important reason for studying the relationship between inputs and output is that the management of an enterprise, public or private, needs to know how much of each commodity to produce. An additional batch of output may not be worth producing. Similarly, additional manpower may not be worth taking on. Additional capital may not be worth employing in the enterprise.

Management must make an intelligent guess as to the most probable sales revenue to be expected from selling various amounts of output. The probable total costs of the various outputs must also be estimated. We are thus dealing with anticipated or planned variables rather than actualities. Of course the plans turn into actualities as time goes on; but expectations are not always fulfilled: expected costs and revenues may change drastically over time. This applies as much to public as to private enterprise.

By taking a definite view about future costs and revenues at various levels of output, management is able to estimate the amount of profit (or surplus in the case of public enterprise) associated with each level of production. It is usual to include under production cost the amount of profit required to keep the particular firm in existence in the industry. This is termed the standard or "normal" profit for that industry. An efficient management, however, would be expected to earn a much greater profit than the "normal" and would therefore select that level of output at which profit was at a maximum. Consider Fig. 3.6, which applies to a business firm producing under perfectly competitive conditions.

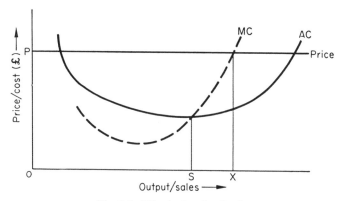

Fig. 3.6 Marginal cost and price

In the diagram the market price is given by OP, and AC is the average-cost curve of the usual "U" shape. A new curve is shown on this diagram. It is the marginal-cost curve MC, denoted by the broken line. Marginal cost is the addition to total cost when an extra unit of output is produced. On reflection it will be seen that fixed cost can have no part in marginal cost since an increment of output will not add anything to the fixed cost. It will add something to the variable cost, however, and this addition is the marginal cost.

Referring to Fig. 3.6 the following points should be apparent:

(a) Management will not plan an output smaller than OS since up to this point each addition to output adds more to revenue than to cost, i.e. marginal revenue is more than marginal cost.*

(b) Thus the "operative" part of the diagram lies to the right of OS where both average cost and marginal cost are rising.

(c) As output is increased from OS to OX each addition adds more to cost than the previous addition; in other words, marginal

---

* This is a slight simplification.

cost is rising. It is worth increasing output, however, to OX, where marginal cost has risen to the point where it just equals price. It would be unprofitable to produce more than OX since beyond this point each addition would cost more than it sold for.

(d) Maximum profitability is at the level of output where marginal cost equals price.

Arguing again from the diagram it can be seen that the firm would break even and make normal profit as long as price covered average cost. Thus the additional profit being earned at output OX would attract new firms into the industry and encourage existing firms to expand output. The result would be a general fall in market price but as long as average cost was being covered the price would be a profitable one. If price fell to the point where output OS was the most profitable output the firm would just make normal profit with price equal to marginal cost and also equal to average cost. At lower prices losses would be made, although in the short run the firm would stay in business as long as total variable costs were being covered. Any greater revenue could be set off against fixed costs.

Fig. 3.6 shows that marginal cost is equal to average cost at the point where average cost is at a minimum. To the left of this point MC is falling faster than AC. To the right of this point MC is rising faster than AC. This is the usual marginal-average relationship. An example will make this clear:

If an output of 9 cost £18 and an output of 10 cost £20
then the average cost of 9 is £2
and the average cost of 10 is £2
Also the marginal cost of the tenth is £2.
But if the output of 9 cost £18 and the output of 10 cost £21
then the average cost of 9 is £2
and the average cost of 10 is £2·1
Also the marginal cost of the tenth is £3 which is greater than the average cost.

These relationships apply to revenue as well as costs. Another name for price is average revenue since it is total revenue divided by output/sales. Marginal revenue is the addition to revenue made by selling one more. Under perfectly competitive conditions marginal revenue also equals price (and MR equals AR as in Fig. 3.6) but as soon as elements of monopoly enter the market situation average revenue diverges from marginal revenue since the management is in a position of being able to influence price by manipulating output/sales. This is an important feature of a monopoly whether public or private. Consider the following revenue position of a monopolist (Fig. 3.7):

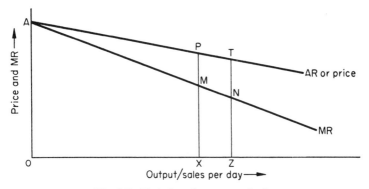

Fig. 3.7 Variation of revenue and sales

When output is *OZ* the average revenue (price) is *ZT* but a knowledge of this market situation may induce the management to contract output to *OX* because by so doing the market price will rise to *XP*. Note that, as sales increase, not only does average revenue fall but marginal revenue falls faster. The revenue earned by selling one more is less than its price since all the previous units must be sold at the lower price too. In the analysis of marginal and average revenues and costs it is assumed that we are referring to output/sales per period of time such as a day, a week or a month. If, in order to increase sales from 10 per day to 11 per day, price has to be lowered from £1 to £0·95 the price or average revenue is now £0·95 but the marginal revenue earned by the eleventh sale is £0·45, i.e. the revenue from selling 11 (11 × £0·95) minus the revenue from selling 10 (10 × £1).

In order to achieve the most profitable output/sales when elements of monopoly are present the rule is to equate marginal cost with marginal revenue. It will always be profitable to sell one more as long as it adds to total revenue more than it adds to total cost. If we

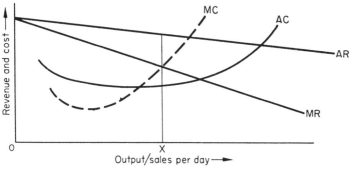

Fig. 3.8 Cost and sales curves

assume that the cost and revenue curves facing the management of a monopolized product were as shown in Fig. 3.8 the most profitable output/sales would be at OX where MC equals MR. The total revenue from selling this output is OX times AR and the total cost of producing this amount is OX times AC. The difference between these sums of money may be termed monopoly earnings. Of course the management may not take advantage of the market situation in this way and may, in fact, produce a larger output where average revenue (price) equals average cost and any possibility of monopoly earnings is forgone.

NATIONALIZED INDUSTRIES

Public enterprise is usually characterized by having considerable monopoly power over the market. Nationalized industries may not only decide on the prices for their products but may also practise price differentiation by charging different groups of consumers different prices. Since fixed costs often form a high proportion of total costs it is usual for production to occur under conditions of decreasing average and marginal costs. Under these conditions marginal-cost pricing will result in a loss which must be covered by the Government out of general taxation. Consider the following diagram (Fig. 3.9):

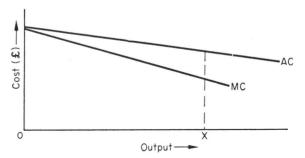

Fig. 3.9 **Decreasing-cost industry**

If output OX is sold at a price equal to average cost, the sales revenue will just cover total cost. Under marginal-cost pricing it will not cover total cost and a loss will be made. The loss may be much larger if the nationalized industry has a statutory obligation to "promote the public interest" in order to take account of what are considered to be important social benefits from having a large output.

On the other hand, if average and marginal cost are rising, the nationalized industry will make a surplus under marginal-cost pricing. This commercial surplus, however, may well disappear if social costs are taken into account and these are high compared with social benefits.

The two-part tariff system of pricing may be utilized by decreasing-cost industries. Note that this system attempts to cover the fixed costs by making a fixed charge to the consumer. The variable cost is then related to the varying charge which the consumer pays.

ECONOMIES OF LARGE-SCALE ORGANIZATION

Economies of large-scale organization, if they can be obtained, will reduce both average and marginal cost. These economies include such items as being able to purchase inputs at relatively low prices owing to buying in bulk; being able to spread administrative and marketing costs over a larger output; taking advantage of large "indivisible" units of capital equipment and introducing greater specialization, mass-production methods and the like.

Large-scale production, however, not only affects the cost side of the equation but also the revenue side. As a business grows large, relative to the other firms in the industry, it may find that it is able to exert an influence on the market, and the larger it grows the bigger is this influence likely to be. In the extreme case the firm may end up in a monopoly position.

Large-scale production usually requires large-scale investment in new capital equipment. When businesses are operating in a small way as sole proprietors, partnerships and small private companies they are usually limited in size by the amount of finance they can raise for capital development. This finance may come from a variety of sources but one of the most important is the retention of profits in the business. With a large organization in the form of a public company it is usual to raise capital from the public by the issue of various types of shares. The usual form of organization for nationalized industries is the public corporation. These public corporations are outside the normal process of company law but they may be allowed to raise capital by selling fixed-interest bonds to the general public. They may, in addition, receive investment funds from the Exchequer. Surplus earnings may also provide them with funds for capital investment.

There has been much argument as to the most efficient way of financing capital investment in the nationalized industries. Investment decisions are closely related to problems of organization. In some nationalized industries there is a tendency to a more powerful central organization. In others the tendency is to apply commercial criteria at much lower levels in the organization so that the lower-level units make their own decisions regarding pricing and investment policy, subject to general policy direction from headquarters. The application to investment projects of management tools such as cost-benefit analysis, discounted cash flow, output-budgeting, etc., results in a more efficient utilization of resources in this sector of the economy.

One of the difficulties with the nationalized industries is that they are all different as far as costs and revenues are concerned. Thus it is impossible to generalize as to what policy should be followed. Those industries working under conditions of increasing cost would earn a surplus if marginal-cost pricing were adhered to. Those operating under decreasing cost conditions would suffer deficits under this pricing policy, but would break even under a policy of average-cost pricing.

Although it can be said that an efficient allocation of resources is brought about by marginal-cost pricing, the imposition of indirect taxes causes prices in the private sector to exceed marginal costs. It may well be that a reasonable allocation of resources calls for a similar balance in the public sector of the economy.

It would seem reasonable to distinguish between the purely commercial criteria and the wider social criteria when decisions are made regarding pricing and investment in State-owned industries. When it is in the public interest to have an operating deficit which is subsidized out of general taxation it could be made clear why this is being done.

QUESTIONS ON CHAPTER 3

1. What is the likely effect on management's output policy of (a) a rising market price? (b) a falling market price? (c) a rise in costs? (d) a fall in costs?

2. (i) Draw a diagram to show that a higher market price will induce management to increase output even though the average cost is rising.

(ii) "As normal profit has been included in AC, it pays to produce more provided it can be sold at a price not less than average cost." Discuss.

3. (i) Marginal cost equals price.
(ii) Price is less than average variable cost.
(iii) Marginal revenue equals marginal cost.
(iv) Price equals average cost.
(v) Average cost equals marginal cost.
(vi) Marginal cost is less than average cost.

Which of these statements are true in the case of decreasing cost enterprises?

A: (iii) only?
B: (i) and (vi)?
C: (v) only?

D: (ii) and (iii)?

E: (vi) only?

4. Which of the above statements are true in the case of a firm making only normal profit in a perfectly competitive market situation?

A: (i) and (vi)?

B: (i) (iii) (iv) and (v)?

C: (iv) and (vi)?

D: (i) (ii) (iv) and (v)?

E: (ii) and (iv)?

5. Which statements are true in the case of a business which is about to close down?

A: (i) only?

B: (i) and (v)?

C: (ii) only?

D: (iv) and (vi)?

E: (vi) only?

6. The following figures show total costs of production and the prices obtained by a monopolist at different rates of output per week:

Output	Total costs £	Price £
9	500	45
10	520	44
11	545	43
12	576	42
13	611	41
14	650	40
15	700	38

(a) What weekly output produces the minimum loss?

(b) What would be the effect on output and price of a subsidy of £10 per unit?

7. Explain how a policy of price discrimination may assist a nationalized industry to overcome the problems associated with a peak period of demand.

8. Do you consider that the pricing and investment policies of nationalized industries should be decided on purely commercial lines?

4 Income, Output and Expenditure

It has already been stated that the public and private sectors of the economy are complementary to each other. Both are concerned with the utilization of scarce resources in the satisfaction of wants. These include public and private wants, collective and individual wants. How can the results of such a complicated economic process be measured? By estimating the national income the economic achievements of one country may be compared with those of another or the economic progress of a country may be assessed over a number of years. Of course some allowance must be made for changes in population, both total, in the sense of the number of mouths to feed, and age-groupings, in the sense of the numbers of pairs of hands available for production in all its aspects. A well-known measure of the results of economic activity over a period of a year is the country's gross national product or G.N.P. It is found by adding up the money values of all the goods and services produced by the country in a year. Money values are used because a common denominator is needed if the outputs of different things are to be aggregated: foodstuffs by weight, textiles by area, liquids by fluid measure, etc. There are three ways of arriving at the same result and these are termed the Gross National Output, the Gross National Income and the Gross National Expenditure.

1. Gross National Output

The economy may be divided into the various industrial sectors such as:

Agriculture, forestry and fishing
Mining and quarrying
Manufacturing
Construction

Gas, electricity and water
Transport and communication
Distributive trades
Insurance, banking and finance
Public administration and defence
Health and educational services
Other services.

Some of these industries are in the private sector of the economy and some in the public sector. They can be found in the annual Blue book on National Income and Expenditure. In this publication are listed the contributions made by each of these industrial sectors to the output of the economy. For example, out of a gross national output of about £40,000 millions, manufacturing accounts for around £14,000 millions and construction for around £3,000 millions. Industrial output (the second, third, fourth and fifth items in the list) accounts for nearly half the G.N.P. whereas agriculture, forestry and fishing (the first item) accounts for about four per cent only.

When all the outputs of goods and services produced in the public and private sectors of the economy are added, the total so obtained is called the *domestic product* since it is produced within the country. This total is really the sum of all the values added at each stage of production, or the contributions to output made by each business organization and enterprise. These net outputs are obtained by subtracting from the value of total output the value of any output purchased from other enterprises, such as raw materials, power supplies, etc. To arrive at the net output of the shipbuilding industry it is necessary to deduct the value of purchases of steel, timber, textiles, engineering and electrical products, as well as services bought from other industries. The result will be the value added by the shipbuilding industry. If this procedure were not followed there would be "double counting" of outputs. The total of all value added within the country is called the Gross Domestic Product (the word "gross" refers to the fact that depreciation has not yet been deducted).

One of the problems associated with the value-added approach is due to the effects of changing prices from year to year. If prices are rising steadily it will appear that output is increasing when, in fact, it may not be increasing in real terms. It is possible for actual physical output to be constant or even decreasing whilst values are rising. Thus it is usual to revalue the outputs at constant prices to eliminate the effects of price changes. After making this adjustment it has been found that the gross domestic product tends to increase at around three to four per cent per annum on average.

Difficult problems arise in measuring the output of services provided by public authorities for the whole community. Many services are provided free of charge and therefore do not have a market price which can be taken as an indication of their value. It is necessary in these cases to utilize other indicators which vary directly with output. For example, the number of teachers employed may be taken to indicate output in education, the number of road-miles covered to indicate the output of the ambulance service.

There is the further problem of how to treat indirect taxes on commodities and services. Subsidies also occur from time to time. In order to value the output "at factor cost", i.e. the value added by the use of resources, it is necessary to deduct indirect taxes and add subsidies, since the former result in market values being higher than actual values and the latter cause market values to be lower.

In addition to the domestic product, the product from abroad (if any) must be added in order to arrive at gross national product. Value added will include those values which are exported anyway. Any deductions to avoid double counting will also include deductions of imported goods and services. This leaves only property income from abroad to be added. Any property income paid abroad is first deducted. (The only other possibility of gaining income from abroad is when the terms of trade become more favourable, i.e. when export prices rise relative to import prices.)

It seems that we are using the terms "output" or "product" and "income" as interchangeable, and so they are. The value of output produced in the economy in a year is the same as the total of incomes of all kinds which are generated in the production of this output. Of course, for this identity to be true, the product must be valued, not at market prices, but at factor cost.

It must be pointed out that the gross national product is a flow of goods and services occurring over the year. One of the things which makes this flow possible is the stock of national capital of all kinds. This capital takes the form of buildings, installations, machinery, vehicles, etc. It would be unwise not to make allowance for the wear and tear on this capital which takes place over the year. A value is therefore placed on capital consumption or depreciation and this is subtracted from gross national product in order to arrive at net national product which is the value of output after allowing for the wear and tear of the nation's capital. (It is usual to include with depreciation an allowance to cover stock appreciation in times of rising prices.) Thus:

	VALUE ADDED by private and public sectors
minus	Stock Appreciation
equals	GROSS DOMESTIC PRODUCT at factor cost
plus	Property Income from Abroad (net)
equals	GROSS NATIONAL PRODUCT at factor cost
minus	Depreciation
equals	NET NATIONAL PRODUCT at factor cost

2. Gross National Income

As was mentioned previously the value of output is the same as the factor incomes earned in its production; thus output can be estimated by aggregating the incomes to which it gives rise.

Income flows, however, include not only receipts such as wages, dividends and rent arising from current output of goods and services, but also the income flows which are not so related. The latter include social-security benefits of all kinds (pensions, family allowances, unemployment pay, etc.) as well as interest on the national debt and gifts. They are called "transfer incomes" to distinguish them from factor incomes arising from current production. As we are measuring the national output these transfer incomes must not be counted in the total. National debt interest is excluded since it relates to the past expenditures of governments and not to the present year's output.

The National Income and Expenditure Blue book distinguishes between income from employment and income from self-employment. It also classifies gross trading profits into those of companies, those of public corporations and those of other public enterprises. Over half the gross national product originates from the activities of registered public companies and private companies. The addition of rent gives the total domestic income, but an allowance is made for stock appreciation in order to arrive at gross domestic income at factor cost. The addition of net property-income from abroad completes the picture of gross national income.

Out of a gross national income of around £40,000 millions per annum about £26,000 millions or over 60 per cent is income from employment in the form of wages and salaries.

In the case of persons working on their own account and in the case of partners in a business their earnings are included with income from self-employment since a precise division into wages, interest on capital and profits cannot be made. Rents are imputed to owner-occupiers in respect of their own houses and they are regarded for income purposes as paying rents to themselves. Where payment in kind is received for services rendered it is included under the general heading of wages. Thus:

	INCOME FROM EMPLOYMENT: wages and salaries
	pay of the Armed Forces
plus	Income from self-employment
plus	Profit incomes earned by companies
	public corporations
	other public enterprises
plus	Rent
less	Stock appreciation
equals	GROSS DOMESTIC INCOME at factor cost
plus	Property income from abroad (net)
equals	GROSS NATIONAL INCOME at factor cost

minus   Depreciation
equals   NET NATIONAL INCOME at factor cost.

There are different ways of dealing with interest and dividends. They form that part of company profits which is distributed to shareholders. If distributed profits are regarded as the incomes accruing to the owners of capital then interest and dividends should be included in factor incomes along with undistributed profits. On the other hand if distributed profits are regarded as transfer incomes paid out of the earnings of companies, then the whole of profit incomes of companies should be included, as it is in the above tabulation.

3. Gross National Expenditure

Income is earned from producing the national output; but this is so because spending takes place. This expenditure is on the consumer goods and capital goods which have been produced. Thus another way of estimating the value of the national output is to aggregate the expenditure on final products. It must be stressed that only final purchases are included; all expenditure on intermediate products, such as raw materials used in production, is excluded, otherwise there would be double counting of purchases.

Consumers' expenditure includes all the expenditure by households on goods and services. The imputed rents of owner-occupiers is included as part of personal expenditure.

The National Income and Expenditure tables separate out the current expenditure on goods and services of public authorities, i.e. central and local government. Their expenditure on capital goods, however, is included with that of private businesses, companies and other trading bodies, under the heading of fixed capital formation. Expenditure on increased stocks is listed separately.

There are two problems connected with total expenditures: the first is concerned with valuation; the second is concerned with foreign transactions. With regard to valuation, the expenditure is taken at the prices actually paid by purchasers. These prices, however, include indirect taxes or taxes on expenditure. Similarly, where subsidies have been given by the State, the expenditure at artificially low prices will not reflect the true value of the output. Thus, from national expenditure at market prices must be deducted indirect taxes, and subsidies must be added, in order to value the expenditure at factor cost.

Foreign transactions are important in an open economy such as that of the United Kingdom. The import-content of final goods generates incomes in countries abroad. Part of total expenditure on home-produced goods originates abroad as payment for exports. If imports are greater in value than exports, some disinvestment will take place in the form of running down gold and foreign currency reserves, an increased indebtedness abroad, or a reduction in assets held abroad. On the other hand, an excess in the value of exports over imports will increase national assets. Thus expenditure on exports is added to domestic expenditure and the value of imports is deducted. Any net property income from abroad is also added in order to arrive at gross national expenditure. Thus:

EXPENDITURE ON CONSUMERS' GOODS
　　　　　　　　　　　　　　by households or individuals
　　　　　　　　　　　　　　and public authorities
plus　　Fixed Capital Formation (gross)
plus　　Increase in Stocks
equals　DOMESTIC EXPENDITURE at market prices
plus　　Exports and Property Income from abroad
minus　Imports and Property Income paid abroad
equals　GROSS NATIONAL EXPENDITURE at market prices
minus　Indirect Taxes, plus Subsidies
equals　GROSS NATIONAL EXPENDITURE at factor cost
minus　Depreciation
equals　NET NATIONAL EXPENDITURE at factor cost.

Out of a gross national expenditure of around £40,000 millions at factor cost, consumers' expenditure accounts for about £30,000 millions.

Whether gross or net estimates are made:

NATIONAL OUTPUT = NATIONAL INCOME = NATIONAL EXPENDITURE.

National output throws light on the flows of production from the various industries in the economy. National income shows the forms which the flows of income can take. National expenditure illustrates how spending is divided between consumers' goods and adding to wealth in the form of capital formation.

Real national income per head is a useful concept for assessing the economic position of a country. Economic efficiency is reflected in the size of the national income in relation to the size of the working population. Changes which are occurring either in output or in population will affect the standard of welfare in the country.

One of the factors affecting the national income is the balance of payments with the rest of the world from participation in international trade.

Let C represent the value of consumer goods produced in a year
Let I represent the value of capital goods produced in a year
Let X represent the value of exports and income from abroad
Let Y represent the value of national income
Let M represent the value of imports and income paid abroad
　(C and I relate to domestic output)

The relation of the balance of payments to national income can then be seen from the equation:

$$Y = C+I+X-M$$

A deficit on the international account reacts unfavourably on the national income of the country.

The distribution of the national income is important from the viewpoint of equity and the stability of the national income is important since fluctuations in it are closely correlated with changes in the level of employment.

Circulation of Income

The simplified diagram, Fig. 4.1, shows how income circulates in the economy. For convenience the number of sectors has been reduced to three: (i) households or personal sector, (ii) production sector consisting of business firms and public corporations, producing consumer goods and services, and (iii) the production sector for capital goods. The broken lines in the diagram show the flows in real

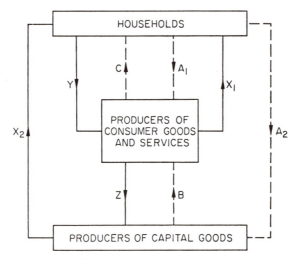

Fig. 4.1 National income, expenditure and output

terms. Households supply labour services as well as the services of land and capital. A_1 and A_2 represent these flows of productive services. The flow of capital goods purchased by the producers of consumer goods is shown by B. Consumer goods purchased by households are represented by C.

The solid lines in the diagram indicate the money flows: X_1 and X_2 are incomes consisting of wages, salaries, dividends, rents, interest payments, etc.; Y is expenditure on consumer goods and services; Z is expenditure on capital goods or investment.

It can be seen from the diagram that national output is represented by B and C. National income consists of X_1 and X_2 and national expenditure is represented by Y and Z.

A_1 and A_2 are the resources used up in production. Allowance must be made for capital consumption, or the gradual wearing out of fixed assets, before changes in income and wealth are assessed.

SOCIAL ACCOUNTING

In the Blue book on National Income and Expenditure accounts are grouped in sectors, each account being concerned with a particular economic activity. Production is the activity reflected in the operating or trading account which shows costs and revenue and gives the balance of profit or surplus. The activity of consumption is indicated in the appropriation account, or income and expenditure account, which shows how the income from the operating account is distributed or paid in taxation. Any income not so distributed becomes savings. The activity of adding to wealth or investment is shown in the capital account where savings carried over from the appropriation account are set off against the acquisition of capital assets. This relationship of the accounts to economic activities is shown as follows:

Social Account	Economic Activity
Operating Account	Production
Appropriation Account	Consumption
Capital Account	Investment

These accounts are drawn up for the various sectors of the economy. Those listed in the Blue book are as follows:

(a) The Personal Sector or Households;
(b) Companies;
(c) Public Corporations;
(d) Central Government;
(e) Local Authorities;
(f) Overseas Sector.

By consolidating certain of these accounts it is possible to show what activities have taken place in the three main sectors of the economy:

(i) Private Sector: consisting of Personal Sector plus Companies;
(ii) Public Sector: consisting of Central Government plus Local Authorities plus Public Corporations;
(iii) Overseas Sector: transactions between residents and non-residents.

The national accounts distinguish between transactions in goods and services, income from property and transfer payments. By careful classification of activities in the various accounts a better understanding of the working of the economy is obtained. One example of this is the preparation of the table of industrial input and output, which breaks down the production sector of the economy into a number of sub-sectors in order to show the flows between them. Where sales by one industry become the purchases of another industry this is shown in the form of a "transactions matrix". This shows to what extent an industry relies on other industries (or on imports) for its inputs of goods and services. A transactions matrix takes the following form:

TRANSACTIONS MATRIX (£ million)

Purchases by:	Agriculture	Chemicals	Motor vehicles	Engineering	Textiles
Sales by:					
Agriculture	—	—	—	—	30
Chemicals	150	—	60	120	25
Motor vehicles	5	2	—	30	1
Engineering	30	90	400	—	20
Textiles	—	8	15	20	—

It shows the interrelationships between the various sectors of the economy and can be used to show changes taking place from one year to the next. For example from this matrix it can be seen that agricultural output of £30 millions became part of the input of the textile industry. This industry also purchased £25 millions of input from the chemical industry, £1 million from motor vehicles and £20 millions from engineering, making a total input of £76 millions. By adding the total of the columns and the total of the rows we get the same result, namely £1,006 millions. From one point of view this total represents industrial input; from another, it represents intermediate output. The matrix can indicate what expansion is required in other industries in order to secure an increased output from a particular industry.

In addition to the various sector accounts and the input-output tables the Blue book also includes financial accounts. These show transactions in financial assets by sector and according to the type of asset. Financial assets include notes and coin, Treasury bills, commercial bills, bank deposits, loans, mortgages, etc. The sectors include banking, insurance, industrial and commercial companies, etc.

When the country is considered as a whole the financial transactions which take place between the residents cancel each other out. The only remaining transactions are those between residents and non-residents, i.e. international financial transactions. This is so because, within the country, financial assets are balanced by financial liabilities; e.g. a bank deposit is an asset to the owner of it but a liability to the bank; a preference share is an asset to the shareholder but a liability to the company issuing it. Thus, although the changes in claims are important for the individual sectors, for the economy as a whole it is the change in overseas net assets that matters.

From the financial accounts the relationship between savings and investment can be seen. Total saving minus stock appreciation plus capital transfers from abroad provides the total funds available for gross investment.

The financial accounts show the savings of each sector and how the savings are used. A particular sector may contribute to capital formation in other sectors by acquiring financial assets issued by those sectors. This means that the other sectors are drawing on the savings of that sector.

Personal savings are used in a variety of ways and the accounts show that two important uses are (a) to provide business capital and investment in housing; and (b) to purchase financial assets such as life assurance, local-authority debt, Government securities, etc.

The funds necessary for investment, or adding to wealth, are provided from the savings of both the public and private sectors of the economy.

It may be asked whether national income is a reasonable indicator of economic welfare. The answer is "yes" provided that changes in population are allowed for, by working out the income per head, and provided that it is the real income of the community which is used in the calculations, and not money income. The real income measures the flow of goods and services becoming available to a country in a year. It gives a useful indication of the economic welfare of the community since income and welfare are directly correlated. It follows that Government decisions which affect the size, distribution or stability of the national income have a direct effect on the nation's economic welfare. Where these decisions affect not only the level of real income but also its distribution the change in welfare is more difficult to determine.

Real national income is found by "deflating" the money value, i.e. by dividing it by an index of the general price level. This index is obtained by taking the level of prices in the base year as 100 and working out the changes in the price level in each subsequent year, in relation to the base year. The following example illustrates the method:

Year	Price	Index
1	50p	100
2	60p	120
3	45p	90

This shows that Year 1 has been taken as the base year with index number of 100. In Year 2 the price has risen by 10p or 20 per cent so the index number is 120. In Year 3 the price has fallen by 10 per cent compared with the base year so the index number is 90.

In obtaining an index of the general price level a large number of typical goods and services is included. Their price changes are "weighted" according to their importance in the community's expenditure pattern. The result is a general price index which can be used to deflate the money value of the national income in order to obtain the real value, relative to the base year. Thus, for the national output, we have:

Money value = Quantity × Price level; and
Real-value or Quantity = Money value ÷ Price level.

In this way, estimates of income, output and expenditure can be revalued at constant prices in relation to a chosen base year.

QUESTIONS ON CHAPTER 4

1. From the Blue book on National Income and Expenditure obtain the latest estimate of gross national product at factor cost and work out the percentage income shares from employment, self-employment, company trading and activities of public corporations. Make a comparison with the estimates of ten years ago and try to explain any significant differences.

2. Select an industry from the input-output transactions matrix in the Blue book and list the industries on which it depends for its inputs, in order of importance.

3. What items enter into the operating account of public corporations (see Blue book).

4. Define "gross investment" and explain its relation to net investment and additions to stocks.

5. If the Gross National Expenditure is £50,000 millions at market prices, and if
    Indirect taxes amount to £8,000 millions
    Subsidies amount to £1,000 millions
    Capital consumption amounts to £4,000 millions
    (a) What is the Gross National Expenditure at factor cost?
    (b) What is the Net National Expenditure at factor cost?

References:
National Income and Expenditure, H.M.S.O.
National Accounts Statistics—Sources and Methods, H.M.S.O.

5　National Output and Income at Full Employment

It has been shown in the last chapter that national income and national expenditure are two ways of looking at the same thing, i.e. national product. What is important, however, for economic welfare is that the national income should be at that particular level which brings about full employment. When real income rises or falls, employment rises or falls. Employment and income move in the same direction. It is total expenditure or effective demand which brings about the production of goods and services and therefore employment. Additional money spent on clothes, for instance, creates more employment and incomes, not only in the clothing industry, but also in many other industries which provide the fixed and variable inputs which the clothing industry utilizes. Nor does the effect stop here. The extra money earned will lead to extra spending and the effect of this will be to create additional income all over the economy. This is the basis of what is called the "multiplier" process. Before discussing this process, however, it is necessary to distinguish various kinds of unemployment and to explain what is meant by the term "full employment".

Unemployment

Since the economy is in a continual state of change with new products coming on to the market and others disappearing, new factories opening and others closing down, prices of some goods rising, of others falling, managers and men changing jobs and new methods of production emerging, it is a wonder that unemployment is not much greater than it is. Some unemployment is obviously inevitable if not essential. It is called "frictional" unemployment and is normally very short-term. Of course if social-security benefits are relatively high and earnings in a particular trade are relatively low this may give rise to a fair amount of voluntary unemployment. Frictional unemployment occurs when small adjustments are taking place in the economy owing to its dynamic nature.

Another type of unemployment is the seasonal variety which occurs in those industries where demand is seasonal rather than at the same level all the year round. Even where vacancies exist in similar occupations in other industries unemployed workers may be reluctant to move. Labour tends to be immobile both occupationally and geographically.

This immobility of labour has been apparent in those areas of the United Kingdom which have experienced regional unemployment of the structural kind. When an industry becomes localized in a certain area the associated labour force tends to become highly specialized to that industry. A fall in demand for the industry's products may have serious consequences for the people living there. Structural unemployment may occur not only as a result of a fall in demand but also because of changes in the techniques of production which lead to changes in the structure of an industry. Depressed areas may emerge, calling for special Government action.

In the United Kingdom, development-area policy has included control over the building of new factories as well as financial assistance to firms setting up business in those areas experiencing regional unemployment.

In addition to unemployment of the structural and seasonal types the United Kingdom, along with many other countries, has experienced a type of unemployment known as "cyclical" unemployment to denote its close association with the trade cycle. Fluctuations in trade involve fluctuations in prices and income as well as fluctuations in employment, and the business cycle can vary in length from a few months to a number of years. It consists of a prosperous phase followed by a phase of depression. The period during which business is making a gradual recovery from the slump is known as the "upturn", whilst the corresponding period in the cycle when boom demand is beginning to collapse is called the "downturn". The cycle is illustrated in Fig. 5.1. In this diagram A and B represent the upper and lower turning points.

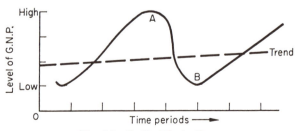

Fig. 5.1 Cyclical fluctuations

The cycle is superimposed upon a general upward trend or growth rate which is shown by the broken line. In the depression national output falls and so do prices and profits. Unemployment rises. In the succeeding period of prosperity national output rises along with prices and profits and unemployment falls. The industries which experience the worst fluctuations are the capital-goods industries such as construction, heavy engineering and shipbuilding. A boom may lead to over-investment in these industries. The resulting excess capacity becomes more noticeable when the depression starts. This excess capacity can only be eliminated by cutting down some replacement investment as well as net investment. A depression may be passed on from one country to another since a serious fall in a community's income will tend to reduce substantially its volume of imports, and thus the incomes of other countries.

The upward trend in G.N.P. on which the business cycle is superimposed may be of the order of two to five per cent per annum, or even more. This growth rate depends on a number of factors of which three important ones are (a) population growth, (b) rate of growth of capital, and (c) the development of technical knowledge including new inventions and their application to industry.

The elimination of the business cycle along with its attendant unemployment is essential if the economy is to follow a stable path of steady expansion in output and income.

Full Employment

By "full employment" is meant the avoidance of cyclical unemployment. Since this type of unemployment is the result of a fall in effective demand, the remedy is to increase the total volume of expenditure.

Other kinds of unemployment, however, require policies of a different kind. Structural unemployment may require work to be brought to the workers in the form of new industries as well as requiring a programme of retraining of the unemployed.

If we define full employment as that state of employment where only frictional unemployment exists, then deviations from full employment can occur as a result of both structural and cyclical unemployment. Thus it can be understood that structural unemployment can exist even though cyclical unemployment has been eliminated. It can exist in times of inflation when the general price level is rising. Full employment is said to be achieved when unemployment is no more than two to four per cent of the labour force. If resources are under-employed then bringing them into use will increase national output and income. Once the point of full employment has been reached, however, output will no longer continue to increase. If incomes continue to increase beyond this point the effect will be to

53

drive up prices and cause inflation. Thus inflation and unemployment are two sides of the same coin. This is shown on Fig. 5.2 where expenditure is measured vertically and output horizontally. *OA* is the full-employment output.

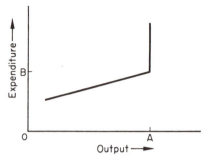

Fig. 5.2   Full-employment output

As expenditure increases in the direction of the arrow, output increases towards *A*, but once this point is reached there is full employment of resources and output cannot increase further in the short term. Thus any further increase in spending beyond *B* will merely serve to drive up prices. Thus it is effective demand which determines the level of output and income in the economy.

THEORY OF EMPLOYMENT

We start with the assumption that the size of G.N.P. is directly related to the level of employment in the economy. When one of these aggregates increases, so does the other. This is a reasonable assumption as, in the short term, changes in population and technical progress can be assumed constant.

The level of employment in the economy, therefore, will depend upon the level of spending. Spending, however, consists of two basic kinds, expenditure on consumer goods and expenditure on capital goods. In a closed economy consumer goods spending plus investment expenditure on capital goods together account for national expenditure which is the same as national income. The effective demand for consumer goods and services will clearly be related to the level of national income. As income increases, so will consumption, because people will be able to spend more money, but the increases in consumption will tend to level out as income goes on increasing. Not all of each additional £1 will be spent; part of it will be saved. It is customary for larger and larger proportions of additional income to be saved as countries grow richer.

This can be seen in the diagram (Fig. 5.3) where *Y* represents national income and *C* represents expenditure on consumer goods and services.

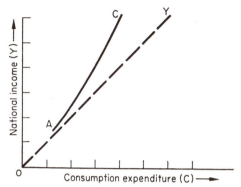

Fig. 5.3 Variation of consumption with income

The broken line (equidistant from each axis) shows the path income and consumption would take if all income were consumed. In fact, consumption expenditure will tend to follow a path such as *AC* as *Y* increases. Average consumption is *C* divided by *Y* so that, if *C* is £30,000 millions and *Y* is £40,000 millions, then average consumption is three-quarters of national income. The fraction of additional national income which is consumed is called the marginal propensity to consume. If *Y* rises by £1 million and *C* rises by half a million then marginal consumption is one-half.

As national income increases, consumption expenditure increases but at a diminishing rate and the difference between income and consumption is saving. Thus saving is a larger and larger fraction of extra income. This is shown by the increasing gap between the broken line and the *AC* line in Fig. 5.3. As income increases the community can afford to save more. Both average consumption and marginal consumption are falling as income rises. Marginal consumption and marginal savings must together account for the whole of any marginal increase in national income. Thus if marginal consumption or *c* is $\frac{3}{4}$, marginal savings or *s* must be $\frac{1}{4}$. In other words, *c* plus *s* equals 1.

The Multiplier Process

The multiplier process was mentioned at the beginning of this chapter. It is necessary to explain this process in some detail since an increase in spending will set this process in motion. The multiplier reflects the fact that an increase in expenditure is passed on to various members of the community in the form of additional income. This additional income is again passed on in the form of extra spending, and so on. This expansionary process comes to an end because there are certain leakages of income, which result in the income not being wholly passed on. Savings is an important leakage. Others are expenditure on imports which creates incomes abroad, and taxation which transfers purchasing power from the community to the Government.

The multiplier process also works in reverse. A reduction in spending will lead to a secondary reduction, a tertiary reduction, and so on, as the effect is passed on. In both an expansion and a contraction of spending the final result will be some multiple of the initial change.

Consider the following example:

Expenditure is stable at £1,000m per week and is all spent on consumer goods. In week 3 an increase in expenditure of £100m occurs, raising total expenditure to £1,100m. If marginal consumption is $\frac{3}{4}$ then in week 4 total expenditure will be £1,075m and in week 5 it will be £1,056·25m and so on. As each week's addition to expenditure is only $\frac{3}{4}$ of that of the previous week, the effect will gradually diminish. This is shown in Fig. 5.4 where time in weeks is measured horizontally and expenditure vertically.

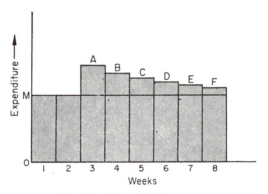

Fig. 5.4 The multiplier process

OM is the normal expenditure of £1,000m per week. Superimposed on this, in week 3, is the additional expenditure of £100m represented by A. The succeeding increments are shown as B, C, D, etc., and each is $\frac{3}{4}$ of the preceding one. Thus it can be seen that, although the additions get progressively smaller, when they are totalled and added to the normal expenditure the result is to increase it by some multiple of the original extra expenditure (A). Just how much is added to total expenditure during the time this process is taking place is found by working out the following:

$$A + \tfrac{3}{4}A + \tfrac{3}{4}(\tfrac{3}{4}A) + \tfrac{3}{4}(\tfrac{3}{4} \times \tfrac{3}{4}A) \text{ and so on.}$$

The answer to this, using the formula for the sum of a geometrical progression, is found to be 4A. Thus the multiplier is 4 in this case and any incremental addition to expenditure will bring about a fourfold increase, given time to work itself through the system. The multiplier can be defined as the reciprocal of the marginal propensity to save. In the example given above

$$\frac{1}{\text{marginal-saving}} = \frac{1}{\frac{1}{4}} \text{ or } 4.$$

Up to now we have assumed that savings leaked out of the system in some way and were lost to the income stream. Thus the induced expenditure gradually became less and less. If new, additional expenditure occurred in each period, however, total expenditure would be maintained at the higher level. There is also the fact to consider that the proportion called savings, which reduces expenditure in one period, may be returned to the system in later periods in the form of investment expenditure. Also, part of "savings" may take the form of import expenditure or taxes to the Government. In both these cases there are losses of purchasing power similar to savings, but there is also the possibility that expenditure may occur in later periods in the form of additional expenditure on exports or additional Government expenditure on goods and services or public investment. Thus the multiplier is really the reciprocal of the sum of marginal savings, marginal import expenditure and marginal taxation, where "marginal" in each case refers to the proportion taken from an extra increment of expenditure or income. The initial expenditure may take a variety of forms. It may consist of consumption expenditure arising from Government grants or tax reductions. It may take the form of extra investment on capital goods from private or public funds. As long as there is an addition to total spending in a particular time period, the multiplier process will be brought into operation.

The Accelerator Relation

Effective demand consists of both consumption expenditure and investment expenditure. The relationship of the latter to the level of national income is not quite so straightforward as in the case of consumption expenditure, since the demand for capital goods is derived from the demand for consumer goods. Thus investment expenditure is related in some way to consumption expenditure. Before investigating this relationship, however, it must be stated that some investment may be independent of consumption in the sense that it is "autonomous" investment rather than induced by changes in consumption expenditure. Three kinds of investment expenditure may be distinguished:

C

(i) replacement of worn-out capital goods;

(ii) autonomous investment in up-to-date machinery in order to produce existing goods more cheaply; and

(iii) induced investment which is the outcome of increased consumption expenditure.

The relationship between a rise in consumption (or a rise in national income) and induced investment is known as the "accelerator" relation. It explains why a period of economic prosperity may come to an end, not because consumption expenditure has stopped rising, but because it has started to level off a little in the sense of having a slower rate of increase. The following example will illustrate this process:

Suppose a factory turning out consumers' goods produces 1,000 articles per week using 50 similar machines. Each machine has an output of 20 per week. If the lifetime of a machine is 5 years, and they are being regularly replaced, the business will purchase 10 replacement machines each year from the capital-goods industry. This replacement investment is the sum total of its investment expenditure as the following table shows:

Year	Consumption demand per week	Machines required	Investment
1	1,000	50	10
2	1,000	50	10

and so on.

Suppose now that in year 3 consumption increases by 400 to 1,400 per week. In order to meet this new demand an extra 20 machines would have to be bought in addition to the normal replacement of 10 each year.

If, in the following year, consumption still increased, but this time by 200 only, and stayed at the level of 1,600 per week, the results would be as follows:

Year	Consumption demand per week	Machines required	Replacement investment	Net investment	Total
1	1,000	50	10	nil	10
2	1,000	50	10	nil	10
3	1,400	70	10	20	30
4	1,600	80	10	10	20
5	1,600	80	10	nil	10

Note that the extra machines which have been bought do not come up for replacement until they have been in production for five years. The important point is that in year 3 a 40 per cent increase in consumption (from 1,000 to 1,400) results in a 200 per cent increase in investment demand (from 10 to 30 per year). The increase in consumption demand leads to a greatly accelerated investment demand.

In year 4, an increase in consumption of just over 14 per cent leads to a decrease in total investment of 33⅓ per cent. This has happened, not because consumption has fallen but simply because its rate of growth has been slowed down. In year 5, even though consumption remains steady at 1,600, investment has fallen by 50 per cent. Of course, in time, the new machines will come up for replacement and total investment will then rise again. If investment in additional machines is spread unevenly over time, recurring cycles of investment demand may occur as replacement becomes necessary.

Thus the accelerator principle refers to the fact that induced investment in any period of time depends on any change in consumption expenditure which has occurred over that period of time. Whereas consumption expenditure varies with income, investment expenditure varies with the rate of growth of income (or the rate of growth of consumption). The actual amount by which investment is induced depends not only on the change in consumption which has taken place but also on the amount of extra capital required to produce a given amount of extra output. This is called the "capital-output ratio". Thus it is not the level of expenditure that affects net investment but the change in that level. Some writers have attributed the business cycle to an interaction between the multiplier, which expands or contracts spending, and the accelerator, which magnifies the effect on the capital-goods industries.

EQUILIBRIUM LEVEL OF NATIONAL INCOME

Whatever the exact relationship between consumption expenditure and investment expenditure, when added together these two make up the national expenditure or income. Since the national income is generated by producing an output of consumption and investment goods, the broken line in Fig. 5.5 represents national income. This line at 45° to the axes shows an equilibrium path where all income is accounted for by expenditure. On this diagram, income is measured horizontally, and expenditure vertically. OO is the supply of output at various levels of national income (Y) and national expenditure (E). Effective demand (D) is made up of consumption demand (C), which tends to level off as income increases, and investment demand (I), which consists of autonomous, replacement and induced investment. Thus by adding C and I vertically, at each level of income, the total effective demand (D) is obtained.

The equilibrium level of national income is OA, where the total demand equals the total output. At this level of income, investment is equal to savings, since the latter is defined as Y minus C. It can be seen from the diagram that savings (the vertical distance from the

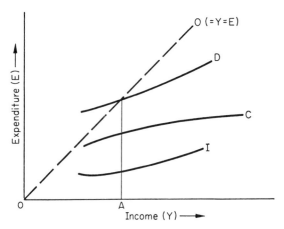

Fig. 5.5 Equilibrium level of national income

C line to OO) equals investment only at the equilibrium level of income, OA.

If income is greater than OA, aggregate demand will be less than aggregate supply and total output will tend to decrease. On the other hand, if income is less than OA, aggregate demand will be greater than aggregate supply and total output will tend to rise. OA is thus a position of equilibrium but, as Keynes pointed out in the *General Theory of Employment*, it may well be an under-employment equilibrium rather than a full-employment equilibrium. If the full-employment output is greater than OA then the economy will not be making full use of its available resources at OA, and welfare will be lower than it could be.

If the full-employment output, however, is less than OA, there will be inflationary pressure in the economy and the excess expenditure will merely drive up prices without being able to expand output further.

The equality of savings and investment in equilibrium follows from the definition of these concepts. If S represents total savings, defined as income not spent on current output of consumer goods and services, then

$$Y - C = S$$

Also, since total expenditure (E) consists of consumption expenditure and investment expenditure:

$$E - C = I$$

But as Y and E are the same, S must equal I.

Savings and investment are equal, although as national income rises or falls they undergo constant change. In order to explain this it is necessary to distinguish two ways of looking at economic concepts. There are *ex-ante* relationships and there are *ex-post* relationships. The former are plans or intentions, rather like the weather forecast; the latter are realities or outturns rather like the actual weather. National income and consumption expenditure relating to last year are outturns whilst a schedule showing what consumption expenditure is likely to be at different levels of national income is a forecast based on the most likely reactions of the community to changes in income.

Supply and demand curves are forecasts but, assuming they are correct and do not change, equilibrium price becomes a reality. It is the only price which actually occurs on the market. In the same way, equilibrium quantity is the only am unt which is actually bought and sold. All the other quantities are what producers and consumers would be likely to supply and demand at the associated prices. These intentions turn into actuality at the equilibrium price.

This distinction between plans and events is applied to economic aggregates such as consumption, investment, imports, exports, and savings. In the case of savings plans and investment plans, the former depend on consumption plans since saving is the difference between income and consumption expenditure. Investment plans are generally made by a different set of people who not only respond to changes in consumption demand (as reflected in the accelerator principle) but who also take account of opportunities for autonomous investment. They are no doubt influenced by the cost of borrowing money (the rate of interest) and by the expected income from the projected investment. The use of "discounted cash flow" analysis may assist them to decide whether a particular investment project is worth while. The important fact is that investment plans and savings plans are made by different sections of the community and there is no reason why these plans should match up. If they do, in fact, match up, then savings and investment will be equal, not only in the planned sense, but also in reality; and at this level of savings and investment, national income will be in equilibrium.

If planned investment is greater than planned savings, this will lead to an increase in spending plans which will drive up the national income until enough extra savings have been generated to meet the additional investment expenditure.

On the other hand, if planned investment is less than planned savings, this will lead to a reduction in spending which will diminish income sufficiently to reduce the amount of savings to equality with the smaller amount of investment spending.

Thus the level of investment spending determines the level of savings in the economy by way of changes in the level of national income.

From the foregoing it can be seen that investment is a crucial factor in the analysis of fluctuations of national income. It would be wrong to conclude, however, that it was the only important factor. In economics, everything tends to act on everything else; therefore it is necessary to isolate certain relationships in order to understand them. The dynamic economy is quite different; there is no isolation, but only the reaction of each component part to every other component part of the system. An advanced analysis would have to take account of a whole set of relationships, some of which are listed below:

Economic concept	*Main influences*
Savings	Income, Interest rates
Investment	Interest rates, Rate of consumption
Employment	Output
Consumption	Income
Imports	Income, Foreign price levels
Exports	Price level, Foreign incomes
Price level	Expenditure, Output

INFLATION AND ITS ECONOMIC EFFECTS

When the general level of prices rises or falls the terms "inflation" and "deflation" are used to describe these changes. They should not be confused with changes in relative prices. A country could have a stable price level whilst, at the same time, movements were going on in relative prices within the system according to the principles of demand and supply. In contrast, the general price level could increase by, say, 25 per cent whilst relative prices remained unchanged. Note that it is relative prices and not absolute prices which remain unchanged.

What causes the general level of prices to rise? The answer may be given in terms of full-employment equilibrium. Once economic activity has reached the full-employment level, output cannot rise further (in the short term) and therefore any further increase in total expenditure will be inflationary: it will cause the general level of prices to rise. The increase in expenditure could be on consumption or investment or both. It could arise from increased money wages resulting in a higher national expenditure, real wages being unchanged. It could arise from an increase in expenditure on exports by foreign countries or from an increase in Government expenditure. The three inflationary components of national income are private expenditure on consumption and investment, Government expenditure, and exports expenditure. By contrast the deflationary components are savings, taxation, and spending on imports. If consumption can be regarded as fairly stable in the short term the various influences can be listed as follows:

COMPONENTS OF NATIONAL INCOME

Inflationary	Deflationary
Investment	Savings
Government spending	Taxation
Exports	Imports

Thus, assuming the economy is in full-employment equilibrium, any tendency for the sum of the inflationary components to increase relatively to the sum of the deflationary ones will cause the general level of prices to rise. It is not just a matter of savings being equal to investment in order to maintain a full-employment equilibrium, but of the inflationary components being offset by the deflationary ones.

The role of money is an important factor in the discussion of inflation. Before dealing with this point, however, we might consider how far inflation is a bad thing. Some writers have argued that a mild inflation imparts confidence to the private sector, as prices are steadily but slowly rising over the years. Profits will be high and future business prospects favourable under these circumstances.

Unfortunately the steady increase in income will lead to an increase in imports, depending on what proportion of extra income the community spends on imported goods. This proportion is known as the marginal propensity to import. It will probably rise as income increases. Depending on the size of the marginal propensity to consume, extra income will also tend to raise the demand for domestically produced goods and services, thus diverting to the home market goods which were previously exported. These changes in expenditure on imports and exports will be reinforced by the inflationary rise in prices which will tend to reduce exports and increase imports, depending on the elasticities of demand and supply. Thus, inflation makes an equilibrium in the balance of payments difficult to attain.

The distributional effects of inflation are well known. All those whose incomes or assets are fixed in terms of money will lose by the fall in its value: as the inflation continues each £ is worth less than before. In so far as wage and salary incomes lag behind the rise in the price level these income-earners will experience a fall in real income. Businessmen tend to gain since they are buying and selling on a rising market. In other words the gap between revenue and costs tends to widen, thus increasing profits. Against this must be set the fact that the businessman's capital will cost more to replace when it becomes worn out.

Inflation is favourable to borrowers of funds but unfavourable to lenders. This is so because when the principle is repaid after so many years it will buy considerably less in terms of goods and services. The

63

Government will gain as a borrower since the interest payments on the national debt will not change. Tax receipts, on the other hand, will tend to rise as prices and incomes rise.

Thus from the distributional viewpoint inflation is inequitable.

Some writers have concentrated on the relationship between money and the general price level. It has been said that if the volume of money is increased when the economy is at a point of full employment, the amount of trade cannot increase, so the full effect will be exerted on the price level, causing it to rise. The theory behind this argument is known as the "quantity theory" and the following equation is based on it:

If M is the quantity of money in the economy (in £s) and V its velocity of circulation (or the number of times each £ changes hands in a year)

and if P stands for the general price-level

and T is the number of transactions or volume of goods and services sold in a year

then the "equation of exchange" is:

$$M.V = P.T$$

or Money × Velocity = Price level × Transactions.
From this equation,

$$P = \frac{M.V}{T}$$

and, provided the number of transactions remains constant and the velocity of circulation does not change, then an increase in the money supply by the "authorities" will lead to a rise in P. In other words it will be inflationary. It is likely that M, V and T will be interdependent, however, and that a change in any one of them will affect the other two. In any case M is determined to a large extent by the banking system and will tend to expand and contract with the level of national income and expenditure. The equation shows that there is likely to be a connection between the quantity of money in the economy and the general level of prices, but it does not explain this relationship; it merely shows that it exists.

QUESTIONS ON CHAPTER 5

1. Consider the following:
   (i) Savings = Investment
   (ii) $M.V = P.T$
   (iii) Marginal savings + Marginal consumption = 1

(iv) $Y = C+I$

(v) Planned investment > Planned savings

(a) Which of the above are true when national income is in equilibrium?

(b) Which of the above are always true?

(c) Which of the above would tend to bring about inflation?

2. Show how the multiplier process and the accelerator relationship may help to explain cyclical fluctuations in output and employment.

3. What is the size of the multiplier if the marginal propensity to consume is $\frac{3}{4}$? What is its size if the marginal propensity to save is $\frac{1}{3}$?

4. "Full employment" does not mean "no unemployment". Discuss.

6   Fiscal Policy

IN economics we must consider both the long-term situation and the short-term situation. The national income must expand over time at a faster rate than population growth if the country's standard of living is to continue rising. The question of what is an appropriate rate of growth concerns the long-term upward trend in output and income. In contrast, the problem of how to achieve a stable economy at full employment without inflation is a short-term problem. Let us consider what the Government can do about it.

If the economy deviates from full-employment equilibrium because of inflationary pressures or owing to developing unemployment, the situation may be stabilized by compensatory fiscal policy operating through the Government's budget. The word "fiscal" refers to the fact that the policy operates through the fiscal instruments of taxes and subsidies. Although the main fiscal changes tend to take place once a year when the budget is presented to Parliament, they can take place at any time, and may take the form of "mini" budgets at fairly frequent intervals.

If total expenditure is insufficient to maintain output at full-employment level there will be a deflationary gap. On the other hand, if total expenditure is greater than that required to maintain full-employment output, an inflationary gap will exist. Fiscal policy may be used by the Government to close these gaps as they arise. In the deflationary case, the Government can provide the additional expenditure which is required. In the other case it can reduce inflationary demand through increased taxation.

It must be realized that policies such as these, acting via Government expenditure and revenue, will result in an unbalanced budget. In the former case the budget would be in deficit, in the latter case it would be in surplus.

The multiplier process means that the initial increment of Government expenditure or reduction in taxation need not be as great as the gap to be eliminated. In very simple terms, if the multiplier is 4 and the gap is £1,000m an initial change of £250m should be sufficient to close the gap. Also, if the change is in consumption expenditure it will lead to induced changes in investment expenditure via the accelerator relationship.

In Fig. 6.1 income is measured horizontally and expenditure vertically. The equilibrium income is *OA* where total expenditure *E* is the same as income, shown by the broken line *Y*.

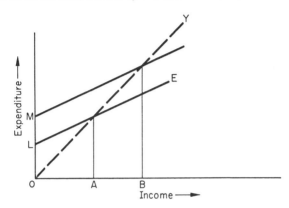

Fig. 6.1   Stabilization policy

If the full-employment income is not *OA*, but *OB*, then Government expenditure equal to *LM* will bring about a new equilibrium at income *OB*. Note that the increase in income is greater than the initial extra Government expenditure which gave rise to it.

Stabilization Policy

Stabilization policy can be achieved in a number of ways. For example, the increase in Government expenditure may be balanced by a similar increase in taxation. This is a balanced budget expansion, with no deficit. The reason it is expansionary is that an additional £1m taken in taxation does not reduce expenditure by £1m since it comes partly out of savings (depending on the size of the marginal propensity to consume). On the other hand, an initial increase in expenditure by the Government of £1m is, in fact, all spent (though the later rounds of spending will be smaller depending on the size of the marginal propensity to consume). Thus, there is an increase in spending of £1m to set against a decrease in spending of less than £1m. The net effect is expansionary.

Stabilization might be achieved by keeping Government expenditure constant and reducing taxation. By this means an expansionary deficit is generated. Not all the gain from reduced taxation will result in expenditure, however. The exact amount will depend on the marginal propensity to consume.

Just as deficit-financing or balanced-budget expansion are useful fiscal instruments for counteracting deflation, so the opposite policies of surplus-financing or balanced-budget contraction may be used to reduce inflationary pressures in the economy. The objective of budgetary policy is to shift effective demand towards full-employment equilibrium.

Suppose that, in Fig. 6.1, OB is the equilibrium income and OA the full-employment income. Then AB indicates an inflationary situation of "too much money chasing too few goods". By budgeting for a surplus equal to ML the Government can channel off the excess demand via taxation in order to achieve the full-employment income of OA.

If we consider net national income as output (O) times the general price level (P) then we can write the following equation:

$$P.O. = C+I+G+(X-M)$$

where C and I are expenditures on domestic consumption and private net investment and G is Government expenditure.

The term in brackets $(X-M)$ refers to income from abroad, X representing exports and income received, M representing imports and income paid abroad.

The left-hand side shows that adjustment can take place in either real output or the price level or both. The right-hand side shows how aggregate effective demand is made up from the component parts. At full employment, O is at a maximum level and if an inflationary gap develops it will simply raise P. This is because there will be a divergence between effective demand in the economy and the value of total resources available in a year. If this difference is in the form of a deflationary gap then O will fall as unemployment rises. It is unlikely in practice for a change to occur in P or O separately. It is probable that relative changes will occur in both. During inflation P undergoes an upward movement relative to O. In a deflation, O undergoes a downward movement relative to P. This follows from the fact that many incomes are fairly inflexible in the downward direction. Trade unions and professional associations tend to resist proposals for wage and salary reductions, so that in a deflationary period the bulk of the adjustment may fall on profits and employment.

Fiscal policy for securing full employment may be direct in the sense of a deliberate adjustment of G; or indirect in the sense of adjustments in taxation and expenditure which will affect C, I or $(X-M)$.

Where stabilization policy relies on adjustments in taxation rather than in expenditure, the initial change will generally have to be greater in order to allow for the community's propensity to consume. Taxation, by altering the amount of disposable income in the hands of the community, increases or decreases expenditure; but the relationship will depend on the size of the marginal propensity to save. There will be a definite relationship between a change in income-tax and the resulting change in expenditure since disposable income will be affected directly. A change in company taxation may achieve the same result through a reduction or expansion of profits; or if passed on to employees, through a change in the rate of increase in wages. Private-investment expenditure may also be affected.

Additions or reductions in consumption expenditure may be effected through adjustments in family allowances, changes in social-security contributions and alterations to subsidies.

It is investment in the public and private sectors of the economy, however, which is the leading factor in bringing about a change in national income and employment levels. Private investment may be influenced by changes in tax allowances for depreciation and by granting special allowances which vary the number of years over which private business capital may be "written off".

The Government may take direct action to alter the pace of public investment. Adjustments to investment programmes in education, housing, roads, etc., and in the nationalized industries, will affect the size of the national income in accordance with the multiplier process. This variation of spending on investment projects is assisted by the preparation of plans well in advance (say, over a period of ten years before completion). They can then be revised annually in the light of general economic conditions.

The term $(X - M)$ may be influenced by import duties and export rebates. Many tariffs are imposed, however, not for the purpose of correcting an adverse balance of payments, but simply to raise revenue for the Government. Under these circumstances it is usual to impose a tax on domestic production of the commodity as well. Where the aim of fiscal policy is to restrict imports in order to achieve a favourable balance of payments, a general import surcharge may be imposed at some percentage of the value of all goods imported.

Automatic Stabilizers

Certain fiscal instruments are themselves stabilizing by reducing disposable income when prices and incomes are rising, and increasing it when prices and incomes are falling. Consider the effect on disposable income of a "built-in" system of unemployment benefits; the nearer the economy moves towards full employment the smaller the transfer of benefits from the State, and the development of unemployment increases the amount of such payments. Thus funds which are accumulated during an inflation are distributed during a depression and the whole process is automatic. Similarly, a progressive tax on income will result in a reduction in tax when there is unemployment and a fall in total wage incomes; and an increase in tax when the opposite obtains. Depreciation allowances based on original cost have the effect of taking more in tax during an inflation when prices are rising and less when prices are falling. Social-security contributions act as stabilizers if they are not payable when a person is unemployed.

In contrast, a commodity tax has to be paid whether the purchaser is unemployed or not. Thus the Government may decide to give power to the Chancellor of the Exchequer to vary rates of tax on commodities including purchase tax. Such a "regulator" may be used at short notice to vary indirect taxes up or down by a certain percentage, thus affecting consumption expenditure.

This brings us to the problem of timing the fiscal changes. If compensatory fiscal policy is to reduce cyclical fluctuations in the economy it must be correctly timed. The automatic stabilizing devices mentioned above go a long way towards bringing this about, but they may be insufficient in magnitude. Thus they need to be supplemented by other fiscal instruments. If a particular Government expenditure is a relatively large part of total Government expenditure then a change in the former will have an important influence on total spending. Similarly a change in a tax which accounts for a large proportion of Government revenue will be an effective means of influencing demand.

If a considerable time lag occurs between the recognition by the authorities that a particular change in policy is required and the effect of that policy on the economy, the result may be to aggravate the situation rather than to moderate it. For by the time the changes in taxation and expenditure begin to be felt the economy may have moved into the next phase of the cycle.

In Fig. 6.2 the broken line shows the long-term trend of full employment income and *YZ* represents the cycle. The fluctuations may be reduced by balancing the budget over the lifetime of the cycle. From year 1 to year 4 a surplus budget would damp down demand and from year 4 to year 7 a deficit budget would expand the level of activity. If, owing to administrative delays and to the fact that income changes take time to work through the economy, there is a time lag of one year or more, the selected policy may lead to a worsening of the situation, since it will be continued into the next phase when policy needs to be reversed.

The policy outlined above is known as "functional finance". It consists of adjustments in both taxation and expenditure in order to

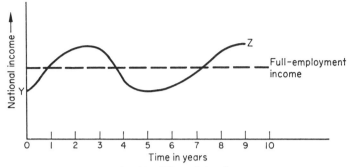

Fig. 6.2 Effect of time lags

compensate for an inflationary or deflationary gap. If the inflationary components of national income are not in equality with the deflationary components, then income will be moving to a new equilibrium which may or may not be a full-employment one. The inflationary components are those which create incomes without creating consumer goods and services for the domestic economy. They are I, X and G representing investment, exports and Government expenditures. The deflationary components are S, M and T representing savings, import expenditure and tax revenue; all these components are income-reducing. Thus, for equilibrium, the inflationary and deflationary sides must balance, giving:

$$I + X + G = S + M + T$$

Budgetary policy may operate directly or indirectly on any and each of these components as well as operating on consumption expenditure. The components are not independent of each other. A rise in I, for example, will generate changes in S, M and T.

It has been said that indirect taxation is a better regulator than direct taxation since the former can be adjusted more quickly than the latter. It must be mentioned, however, that some indirect taxes may change the amount of spending by nearly the full amount of the tax, whilst others change it by only a very small amount. Taxes placed on articles consumed mainly by the higher-income groups are likely to be paid partly out of savings. This would not be likely to apply to taxes on goods consumed mainly by the lower-income groups. Generally, taxes on spending will be more effective in changing aggregate expenditure than taxes on income since these also tax the part of income which is saved.

The Government must estimate the annual flow of exports and income from abroad in order to compare this with planned foreign investment and probable flow of imports. Taxes and transfer incomes must be forecast as well as domestic income and consumption.

Planned savings may be estimated, both public and private, and compared with total investment to indicate the size of the "gap".

In spite of the seeming simplicity of the relationships quoted, much fiscal policy is likely to be of the "trial and error" type since there is so much uncertainty about the future in a dynamic economy. What are the economic indicators which the Government must take note of? In an open economy like that of the United Kingdom the balance of payments must come high on the list. This means that such aggregates as imports, exports, property income paid and received from abroad, foreign short- and long-term borrowing and lending, must be estimated at frequent intervals and any changes noted. Movements in the balance of payments are reflected in pressures on the external value of the currency and in changes in the country's reserves of gold and foreign currencies.

Another important indicator is the proportion of the labour force which is unemployed. The ratio of unfilled vacancies to unemployed workers may give a reasonable indication of the level of employment in the economy. Full employment may be defined as an agreed percentage of employment so that deviations either way would indicate either the development of inflation or of deflation.

Price-level stability may be difficult to achieve in times of full employment, since, if wages and other costs are inflexible in a downward direction, the pressure is continually upwards on prices. There are various index numbers of price levels which indicate the rate at which prices are rising or falling.

The overall annual change in gross domestic product at factor cost and its division between private investment and consumption and public investment and consumption is published by the Government in the *Financial Statement and Budget Report* each year. Changes in national income components and credit supply are reported monthly in *Economic Trends* prepared by the Treasury.

GROWTH OF THE ECONOMY

Fiscal policy is not simply concerned with the maintenance of full employment whilst at the same time securing a desirable allocation of resources and an equitable distribution of income and wealth. It must also be concerned with the rate of economic growth. This is the long-term upward trend in national income and output—not in monetary terms but in real terms. Balanced growth is based on a proper relationship between economic variables. Some of the more important of these are (*a*) the rate of increase of the population, (*b*) the ratio of capital to output, (*c*) the relationship of savings to investment and (*d*) technical progress.

(*a*) *The rate of increase of the population.* All plans in the private and public sectors must take account of this. Future trends are estimated, not only of the population as a whole, but also of the various groups within it. These include the working population, the school population and the population of retired persons.

Population estimates are based on assumptions regarding future birth and death rates, immigration and emigration rates; and are related to the present size and age-distribution of the population.

(b) *The ratio of capital to output.* This is called the "capital–output ratio" and signifies the marginal addition to the stock of capital goods necessary to produce a marginal addition to real output. A low capital–output ratio is to be preferred to a high one, since if it is low a small amount of investment will raise output a great deal. Investment is important for two reasons: it increases the productive capacity of a country by adding to its capital resources; it also increases national income and expenditure. For balanced growth the increase in capacity must be in step with the increase in income.

(c) *The relationship of savings to investment.* Savings is generally assumed to be a constant proportion of national income. Investment, on the other hand, in so far as it is income-determined, is likely to be induced by changes in income from one period to the next.

If Y_0 represents last year's national income and Y_1 represents this year's, then the change in income from last year to this year is

$$(Y_1 - Y_0)$$

and if total investment in year 1 is some proportion of this change, say g, then:

$$I_1 = g(Y_1 - Y_0)$$

Savings, however, is assumed to be a constant proportion (s) of national income in the same year, i.e.

$$S_1 = s.Y_1$$

In order to have balanced growth, savings and investment must be equal; thus the right-hand sides of these equations must equal each other, viz.

$$s.Y_1 = g(Y_1 - Y_0)$$

from which the following relationship is obtained by dividing both sides by g:

$$\frac{s}{g} \cdot Y_1 = Y_1 - Y_0$$

which shows that, if s and g are constant proportions, so also will be $\frac{s}{g}$ and thus, for balanced growth, national income must change by

73

this constant proportion from one period to the next. This is the balanced rate of growth which is warranted by the proportions *s* and *g*, and is therefore sometimes called the "warranted" rate of growth. It can be upset by either a change in the capital–output ratio or a change in the propensity to save, or both. In order to have balanced growth in the economy, national income must not only be increasing but it must be doing so at an increasing rate.

(*d*) *Technical progress*. This depends on such things as inventions and innovations, new production processes, the discovery of new products and materials. To some extent this goes on all the time because as machines come up for replacement they are often replaced by improved versions incorporating all the latest devices.

When growth is taken into consideration by the Government in framing its current fiscal policy it is found that there are many problems to consider. Growth in investment expands the productive capacity of the economy, and is thus instrumental in producing additional output. At the same time, any extra investment must act as an offset to extra savings, otherwise there will not be an equilibrium. The Government has a choice between different growth rates. By curtailing consumption expenditure and increasing public investment it could step up the rate of growth considerably. The actual rate of growth may be quite different from what is considered appropriate. There is also the concept of the "natural" rate of growth which is in accordance with the rate of change of population as well as non-human resources. If this natural rate of accumulation is greater than that of which the economy is capable, given the degree of voluntary saving in the community, then there will be continued inflationary pressure. Alternatively if saving is higher than required investment at the natural rate there will be continued deflationary pressure. There is thus a close connection between the rate of growth and cyclical fluctuations in the economy, and fiscal policy which affects one will obviously affect the other.

Total investment growth may be accelerated or slowed down by international payments. An excess of exports over imports is a type of investment, whereas an excess of imports over exports is a form of disinvestment. Thus a favourable balance of payments not only helps to expand income; it also helps to offset savings. Fiscal policy which is directed at altering the external situation will indirectly affect the rate of growth.

In the United Kingdom, the National Economic Development Council has been concerned with the appropriate rate of growth and the methods of achieving it. The tendency for wage incomes to increase at a faster rate than productivity, thus leading to inflation, resulted in a Government "incomes policy" with the objective of holding the annual increase in income in step with the annual increase in productivity. A rate of growth of output of four or five per cent per annum has been regarded as a satisfactory target.

A full-employment policy underlines the fact that if resources are being fully utilized then more investment can only take place by having less consumption. This fact has been recognized by collectivist economies where growth has been encouraged by deliberate policies of "forced" saving through high taxation, or by a planned reduction of consumption in order to increase investment. Forced saving may take place in a mixed economy too, especially when it is desired to secure an increase in public investment. In nationalized industries there are many opportunities for public investment. Capital accumulation may also be encouraged by stimulating private investment through tax concessions or subsidies. Fiscal policy, by affecting the propensity to consume, automatically affects the propensity to save, although tax and expenditure changes may affect savings directly. Expenditure on education and health affects the rate of growth if it changes the productivity of labour. Technical progress may be stimulated by Government expenditure which encourages research and the application of scientific discoveries and inventions to production.

By all these means, fiscal policy may assist in the achievement of a balanced rate of growth. It must be remembered, however, that in the mixed economy progress depends on the enterprise and foresight of businessmen. Thus it is important that the Government should provide, as far as possible, conditions which are favourable to economic growth in both the private and public sectors of the economy.

QUESTIONS ON CHAPTER 6

1. If aggregate demand at full-employment income is £50,000m and estimates of planned spending give a total of £60,000m, by how much should the budget be in surplus to close the inflationary gap if the marginal propensity to consume is $\frac{3}{4}$?

2. What is meant by "public investment"? What will be the likely effect of changes in the amount of public investment on the level of employment in the economy?

3. "The speed of economic growth depends more upon the rate of accumulation of capital than upon the growth of population." Discuss.

4. Consider the following items:
    (a) an increase in the level of taxation of consumer goods;
    (b) a redistribution of income from rich to poor;
    (c) a deficit budget;

(*d*) a fall in the propensity to save;

(*e*) more generous depreciation allowances.

(i) Which item(s) would be likely to have an expansionary effect on the economy?

(ii) Which item(s) would tend to increase private investment?

(iii) Which would be useful in curbing inflation?

(iv) Which would tend to bring about a rise in total savings?

7 Economic Policies

IN the last chapter we looked at some of the ways in which the Government may use the fiscal instruments of taxation and expenditure to assist in the management of the economy. In this chapter we shall note other instruments of control and, in particular, monetary and debt policy.

One of the aims of Government is to maintain full employment without inflation. This objective may be frustrated if money incomes are allowed to grow at a faster rate than output is growing. To prevent this happening the Government may institute an "incomes policy" which tries to keep increases in wages and profits in step with productivity growth in order to avoid inflation. If employment is already at a high level, a general rise in wages, unaccompanied by a matching increase in productivity, can lead to a cost inflation. One of the difficulties with which the policy tries to deal is that the demand for higher wages stems not only from the attempts of trade unions to keep in step with each other, but also from the fact that price rises upset the distribution of income between the various social groups in the economy. If rival unions are forcing up wages, this may lead to an attempt to retain the share of profit incomes by raising prices. Thus deviations from full-employment equilibrium may arise because of action in the wage and profit sector. If the Government is responsible for maintaining equilibrium in the national income at full employment, and this is threatened from any quarter, then it can be argued that suitable action should be taken to regulate the situation. Hence an incomes policy may be necessary from time to time. All proposals for wage increases may be examined by a "prices and productivity board" set up by the Government. The board may decide whether the proposed increases should be allowed and it may suggest maximum permissible increases in the light of an industry's productivity.

The growth of monopoly may also work against the attainment of full employment if there is considerable restriction of output. Governments have therefore formulated "monopoly policies" to control the development of large single-firm monopolies and to regulate the growth of monopolistic agreements between firms.

Special Government policies may also be required in connection with the location of industry, especially where the decline of staple industries has led to serious unemployment. These policies may be executed by the central Government itself: as for example when it has power to buy land and build new factories in certain areas or to give financial assistance to firms moving there; or they may be executed by Government agencies or local authorities who may be given special powers with regard to industrial development.

The international balance of payments position has been shown to be an important influence on the national income and thus on the attainment of full employment. Government policy which is directed towards the achievement of an international balance includes such instruments as tariffs, surcharges, quotas, export subsidies and a change in the external value of sterling by means of devaluation or revaluation.

MONETARY POLICY

In the highly developed economy money is of fundamental importance not only because of its own usefulness but because without it there would be little or no specialization and division of labour and therefore none of the advantages that accrue from them. Money functions as a medium of exchange and a common denominator in which values can be expressed. It is also a store of value although its effectiveness in this respect is dependent upon reasonable stability in the general level of prices. Money also exerts considerable influence on the level of activity in the economy via the effect of rising and falling prices. It is necessary, therefore, for Governments to act through the banking system, from time to time, in order to vary the amount and the price of money and credit in the economy. Such action is referred to as "monetary policy".

The important part played by money in the economy may be explained by highlighting the various reasons why money is in demand. If we consider the aims of a business enterprise it will be seen that the most important one is profitability, which depends on the difference between revenues and costs over the accounting period. There is a further objective, however, and that is what management regards as an appropriate structure of assets both liquid and non-liquid. This classification corresponds very roughly to monetary and non-monetary assets. Money is the most liquid asset but very short-term loans and bills of exchange which have been discounted come in second place. Liquid assets are not all in the form of ready cash or money at the bank. What then are the reasons for holding liquid assets, and in particular, for holding money? It is possible to distinguish three motives:

(a) The transactions demand for money arises from the fact that receipts and payments do not coincide. There is a time lag between the revenue coming in and the payments being made from it. In industry, the greater the number of firms, the more money will be required to effect the necessary transactions between them. In times of inflation the higher prices will mean higher money values and thus more money will be required. This tendency will be strengthened by the rising volume of activity up to the full-employment equilibrium. During a depression less money is required since not only are prices falling but so is the volume of trade. Households as well as enterprises demand money for a similar reason. Their incomes accrue each week or each month but they are disbursing their income in the form of expenditure more or less continuously. The less frequently "pay day" comes round, the larger the money balances will have to be in order to finance the necessary transactions. Thus in the normal processes of production and consumption a stock of money is required in order to finance the associated receipts and payments. If this money were not available, households and enterprises would be unable to pay their debts as they became due. The transactions demand for money varies with national income.

(b) The "uncertainty" demand for money, sometimes called the precautionary motive for holding money, arises from the fact that the economy is a dynamic one so that reserves must be held to meet unforeseen contingencies. These reserves may not all be in the form of money; they may include non-liquid assets such as stocks and shares in various companies. The money part of these reserves provides immediate liquidity and is a kind of insurance against unforeseen circumstances. Like insurance it has a price. The price is the interest which it could have earned had it been used to purchase financial assets, such as bills of exchange, Treasury bills or Government securities. Money which is held for reasons of uncertainty is not part of the normal monetary circulation but is said to satisfy the desire for liquidity. This is also true of the third reason for demanding money.

(c) The speculative demand for money is based on expectations of future trends in the economy. If prices are expected to fall the demand for money will rise since it can be used to purchase commodities and services later, when their prices have fallen. Since this money demand is based on expectations it will also be affected by the way the prices of securities are changing. When prices are rising generally the demand for money will tend to fall since it is depreciating in value.

The demands for money listed under (b) and (c) are often referred to as "hoarding", since the money is withdrawn from the active circulation and takes the form of idle balances.

If the Government increases the amount of money in the economy the holders of money balances will feel that their balances are in excess of what they require. They will therefore tend to spend them on goods and services, thus adding to effective demand. Once full employment has been reached, prices will rise until there is an equilibrium between the increased supply of money and the various demands for money. This policy is an expansionary one and is based on the monetary side of the economy. The reverse policy would call for a reduction in the amount of money, thus stimulating holders of money balances to augment their holdings by reducing expenditure until a new equilibrium was reached in the downward direction.

Control over the monetary system is exercised by the Government and Treasury through the central bank and the country's banking system. In the United Kingdom the Bank of England is a public corporation like the Post Office. It works closely with the Government, acting as its banker and advising it of changes in economic conditions in the domestic and international spheres. The Bank is the sole note-issuing authority (apart from a small issue from Scottish and Irish banks). The notes are not backed by gold; they are described as a "fiduciary" issue, i.e. they are backed by Government securities. Out of about £4,000 million notes outstanding, £3,000 million is held by the general public. The Bank of England is also banker to the commercial banks who transact most of the banking business with the public. They hold part of their cash reserves at the Bank of England, the remainder being held in their own tills; usually the division is about 50 per cent in each. The commercial banks' cash reserves form about 8 per cent of their total deposits. This is called their "cash ratio". In addition they hold about 28 per cent of their assets in liquid form such as cash, money lent at very short notice, trade bills and Treasury bills. This is their "liquidity ratio". Their non-liquid assets consist of investments and advances.

Other financial institutions which are concerned with the supply and demand for credit are the money market with its discount houses and merchant banks and the capital market with the Stock Exchange, issuing houses, insurance companies, building societies, etc. The former institution is a market for short-term loans; the latter is a market for long-term loans. Both markets are concerned with new issues as well as existing debt. Rates of interest in both markets may be influenced by the central bank.

INTEREST RATES

Monetary policy seeks to influence the level of activity in the economy by acting on the supply of money and liquid assets both directly and indirectly by means of changes in rates of interest. The Government through the central bank may purchase or sell securities in the market (this is known as open-market operations). Note the fact that Government securities are fixed-interest securities. Interest is not the same as "yield". The yield depends on the price paid and the latter fluctuates inversely with interest rates. If interest rates in general are rising, prices of fixed interest bonds will tend to fall so that their yields are kept in step with the yields on newly issued securities which carry higher rates of interest. Lenders try to obtain the best terms they can for their money; thus, if the Government is forcing down the yields on securities by purchasing them in the open market and so driving up their prices, there will be a tendency for all other yields to fall, including the rate of interest on new issues.

Similarly, if the Government is selling securities to the public this will tend to lower their prices and raise their yields, thus helping to force up rates of interest. If bank rate is changed in the same direction this will reinforce the movement.

Credit expansion involves a general lowering of interest rates and credit restriction a general raising of rates. The Bank of England may supplement its action in the market and on bank rate by issuing directives to the commercial banks or by requiring them to leave part of their cash reserves in "special deposits" at the Bank where they are divorced from the normal cash of the banks.

Since the banking system works to a cash ratio of 8 per cent, the Bank of England by purchasing or selling securities can influence the size of the banking system's cash reserves at the central bank. Therefore it can alter the amount of bank money in the economy since this is about $12\frac{1}{2}$ times the cash base with a cash ratio of about 8 per cent. When the Government sells securities to the public, cash is transferred from ordinary bank accounts to the Government's account, thus reducing the volume of cash in the economy along with the infra-structure of credit which was based on it. Similarly, the purchase of securities by the Government will tend to release cash into the economy and expand the credit which is based on it.

Bank money is by far the most important part of the money supply. If currency in circulation stands at, say, £3m then clearing-bank deposits (current and deposit accounts) will tend to be about £11m. Monetary policy may affect both these components. This strategy includes, in addition to open-market operations, changes in bank rate, special deposits and the issue from time to time of directives to the commercial banks. Although the effect of monetary policy on the

81

domestic economy is not precisely predictable, since additions to the money supply may simply find their way into liquidity holdings rather than be translated into effective demand, it is a useful instrument for the Government to have in support of fiscal and other policies. It is probable that monetary policy is more efficient in restricting the economy in time of inflation than in giving it a boost in times of under-employment of resources.

One of the disadvantages arising from this is that, if monetary policy is used mainly as a restrictive device to counter inflation, and fiscal policy is used mainly as an instrument of expansion (since tax-reductions are popular), then high interest rates are likely to be a continuing feature of the economy. As a result the rate of capital accumulation and thus the growth rate of the economy may be slowed down.

Interest rates affect investment projects via the cost of borrowing loanable funds. In economics "investment" means accumulation of capital resources. The word is used generally to mean "putting money into something" such as an investment trust or a football pool. Much of what is commonly called investment is really the transfer of ownership in existing securities and is thus unconnected with current output. Whether the loanable funds coming on to the capital market will in fact be borrowed depends on whether the rate of return which is expected from putting them to use is greater than the cost of borrowing the funds. This cost is related to the current rate of interest. The more credit there is available, the lower the rate of interest is likely to be, but on the other hand, however low interest rates have fallen, investment may not be stimulated unless expectations of rates of return are good. The further investment decisions extend into the future, the greater will be the degree of uncertainty.

Management must compare the expected rate of return on new capital projects with the cost of borrowing the investment funds. The rate of return depends on what the flows of income from the project, over its lifetime, add up to in total. If the return exceeds the rate of interest (which is the cost of borrowing) then the investment will be worth while. Thus a change in interest rates is likely to bring about an inverse change in investment. What business firms need to know is the present value of the stream of income from the investment project, discounted back to the present. The rate of discount which makes the present value of the income-stream equal to the present cost of the investment project is called the "marginal efficiency" of capital. As long as the rate of interest is less than this it will pay business firms to borrow money and invest in new projects. Discounted cash flow analysis is a method which assists management to decide on the "worthwhileness" of an investment plan. For example, if by investing £420,000 cash inflows of £169,000 are expected over the lifetime of the investment, which is, say, three years, then the rate of return is found by evaluating x in the following equation:

$$£420,000 = \frac{£169,000}{(1+x)} + \frac{£169,000}{(1+x)^2} + \frac{£169,000}{(1+x)^3}$$

In this example x works out to be approximately 0·1 or 10 per cent. Thus the investment is a worth-while proposition provided the rate of interest (the cost of capital) is less than 10 per cent. A rise in the rate of interest above this figure would tend to increase the number of capital projects "in cold storage".

When there is excess capacity in the economy, a fall in interest rates may not result in much additional investment since output can be expanded from existing excess capacity. Also many capital projects are in the nature of long-term engagements and may not be sensitive to interest-rate changes once these projects have been started. In the public sector, the criteria on which investment decisions are based may or may not take account of the existing structure of interest rates, but the Treasury test discount-rate may be used.

Monetary policy is complementary to fiscal policy. It can exert control over interest rates, bank lending and liquidity. If this policy is pushed too far, however, there is a danger that other (non-bank) financial institutions may perform some of the traditional functions of the banking sector and to this extent the performance of the monetary instruments will be weakened.*

In the sphere of international trade monetary policy is possibly more predictable in its effect. A relative change in rates of interest between countries will probably result in a flow of funds from the relatively low to the relatively high interest-rate economies. Confidence, however, is as important as interest-rate differentials in attracting short-term funds from overseas, but what is regarded as a "correct" monetary policy by foreign investors may well strengthen the external value of a country's currency.

THE NATIONAL DEBT AND GOVERNMENT BORROWING

The National Debt of the United Kingdom totals around £36,000m and consists of about £21,000m of Government securities (gilt-edged stocks) and about £6,000m of outstanding Treasury bills; the rest being in the form of National Savings of various kinds. These figures fluctuate from year to year as also does the external debt which varies from £2,000m to £3,000m and consists of that part of the debt which is in the hands of foreign holders. When this part is serviced, i.e. by

---

* New arrangements on banking competition and control came into force in autumn 1971.

making the interest payments, there is a flow of income abroad which may be converted into gold or foreign currencies, thus exerting pressure on the external value of sterling. The higher the rate of interest, the larger the outflow of income payments. This was stressed in the *Report of the Committee on the Working of the Monetary System* (Cmnd. 827, H.M.S.O.).

The National Debt increases when the Government is borrowing additional money from the public. This occurs when there is a deficit in the Government budget because expenditure is in excess of revenue. The Debt falls when the budget is in surplus. This may allow the Government to repay part of the Debt.

It is not only a budget deficit that causes the National Debt to increase, however. It may rise because the public sector is growing. When private-sector industry is nationalized and the shareholders are given Government securities in place of their shares the National Debt will rise. The most important reason for an increase in the Debt is found in the expenses of wartime. When a country engages in a major war the National Debt increases at an accelerated rate.

The National Debt of the United Kingdom includes both marketable and non-marketable debt. Marketable debt accounts for about eighty per cent of the total and is divided between long-term, medium-term and short-term debt. The long-term debt is composed of Government stocks with a life of over five years to maturity, although some of these stocks are undated. As time goes on the dated stocks become medium-term debt with a life of from three months to five years to maturity. The short-term debt is composed of Treasury bills with a life of up to three months. Rates of interest are fixed on Government bonds from around $2\frac{1}{2}$ per cent to around $9\frac{1}{2}$ per cent but the market tends to equalize their yields through the emergence of different equilibrium prices. The other twenty per cent of the National Debt is in the form of non-marketable debt consisting of national savings, tax-reserve certificates, notes held by the International Monetary Fund, etc.

Undated debt is sometimes called "funded" debt. The Government is under no obligation to repay it. In contrast, "unfunded" debt is composed of long- and medium-term debt with a repayment date which averages about thirteen years. Treasury bills run for three months before maturing. They are issued by tender to the London Money Market each week, although a portion of the issue goes "on tap" to Government departments with funds to spare for short-term loans. Treasury bills, along with "ways and means" advances from the Bank of England to the Treasury together form what is known as the "floating" debt.

Nearly thirty per cent of the National Debt is in the hands of "official" holders, i.e. the National Debt Commissioners and the

Bank of England. The former hold Government securities on behalf of the national and trustee savings banks (ordinary accounts) and national insurance funds. The latter holds government securities as backing for the notes issued by the Bank of England Issue Dept.

Of the remaining seventy per cent or so of "non-official" holdings a sizeable proportion of debt is held by the banking and financial sector. Assuming the National Debt is around £34,000m a typical breakdown is as follows:

U.K. NATIONAL DEBT

		£m
Official Holdings:		
National Debt Commissioners and Government Depts		
Bank of England Issue Dept and Exchange Equalization Account		10,000
Non-Official Holdings:	£m	
Banking sector	3,000	
Insurance companies	3,000	
Building societies, Pensions funds, Savings banks (investment accounts)	2,000	
Industrial and commercial firms, etc.	4,000	
Private individuals	5,500	
Overseas residents	6,500	24,000
		34,000

Of this total, the last item represents a liability to the rest of the world. It constitutes pressure on the balance of payments in the form of "unrequited" exports. As far as the rest of the debt is concerned "we owe it to ourselves". In other words, the interest payments are transfer incomes paid from taxation to the current owners of debt. Thus, apart from the externally held debt, it can be argued that there is no burden on the community. In any case a fair proportion of the debt is held by the Government and banking sector of the economy.

It is a fact, however, that, when the debt increases, extra taxation is required for the additional interest payments and this may have disincentive effects on current output of consumer and capital goods. In so far as investment is retarded, future generations inherit a smaller stock of capital than they might have done. Had the additional deficit been tax-financed there would have been no debt to service. Where debt interest is paid there is a redistribution of income from taxpayers to holders of debt and to this extent future generations are affected. It may also be argued that, if there is an addition to gilt-edged securities at the expense of industrial shares, the rate of private investment is slowed down; and in so far as this is not compensated by additional public investment the rate of growth of national income may be affected adversely. This burden is reflected

85

in the smaller amount of real capital added to the existing stock which is passed on from generation to generation.

Of course there may be times when a Government deliberately chooses to finance a deficit in its budget not by fiscal means such as reducing expenditure or increasing taxation but by borrowing and thus increasing the size of the National Debt. This might be the case, for example, when stability is the objective of the Government in times of unemployment. A growth in the debt is, under these circumstances, a necessary adjunct of fiscal policy.

At other times, the composition of the debt may be changed in order to increase or decrease the volume of liquidity in the economy. For example, if fewer Treasury bills are issued and their place is taken by additional issues of long-term securities, the volume of liquid assets in the economy is thereby reduced. This action is generally an adjunct of monetary policy.

Thus debt policy forms a link between fiscal policy and monetary policy. There are certain problems, however, regarding the absolute size of the National Debt in relation to national income. One of these is that the existence of a large debt may incline the Government to follow a policy of low interest rates so that the cost of servicing the debt is relatively small. In this case a conflict arises in times of inflationary pressure on the economy for, on the one hand, low rates of interest are required in order to economize on expenditure, and on the other hand, high interest rates are required in order to operate a "credit squeeze".

Another problem is concerned with inflation. Since the Government's commitments for servicing and redeeming the debt are fixed in money terms, inflation will have the effect of increasing money incomes and thus reducing the burden of servicing the debt. There is thus an inducement to Governments to acquiesce in continuing inflationary conditions.

A third problem associated with the redemption of Government securities when they mature is that their owners may prefer to add to their expenditures rather than to re-purchase gilt-edged stock. In this case the redemption of debt will result in inflationary pressure.

Additional Government borrowing may itself be inflationary if it leads to Government spending of money which would otherwise have been "hoarded" in the sense of satisfying liquidity preference. If this happens during unemployment, however, the increase in output will tend to be much more important than any rise in prices. Government expenditure will also be an addition to total spending if it comes from new bank credit which has been lent to the Government by the banking system.

When additional Government borrowing forces up interest rates private investment may fall off. In so far as the money comes out of expenditure the effect will be similar to a credit restriction. Thus it is difficult to say whether additional Government borrowing is inflationary or deflationary until all the circumstances are known.

Non-official or market holdings of debt may change owing to changes in official holdings. Part of these are in the hands of various Government departments with funds to spare for the time being and another part finds its way into the Exchange Equalization Account of the central bank. The purpose of the Account is to assist in maintaining the external value of sterling when there are upward or downward pressures upon it. The Account aims to maintain its value within the limits agreed with the International Monetary Fund.

By purchasing sterling when its external value is falling in terms of other currencies, and by selling sterling when its value is rising, the Account functions as a stabilizing agent. By operating through the supply and demand mechanism in this way the Account assists in keeping the price of sterling within the official range. When the Account sells sterling it adds to its stock of gold and foreign exchange. It obtains the sterling by converting some of its holdings of Government debt. When the Account buys sterling it loses gold and foreign exchange. Its additional sterling is then converted into Government debt (Treasury bills and Government stock). This debt forms part of the official holdings. Since the country's gold reserves are held in the Exchange Equalization Account, continuing pressure on the £ weakens the reserves.

The relation between fiscal-policy, monetary-policy and the national debt is shown in highly simplified form in Fig. 7.1.

A budget deficit may be financed in a number of ways and various methods may be used at the same time. If the deficit is financed by borrowing the National Debt will increase. On the other hand, if the deficit is financed by printing and issuing new money the debt will not increase. Debt which is held in the central bank is part of official holdings and is not therefore regarded as part of market holdings.

A budget surplus may be financed by reducing the money supply or by redeeming part of the National Debt. Both of these may occur at the same time. The problem with varying the money supply is that an increase is inflationary when the economy is nearing full employment and changes in the money supply are normally complementary to changes in rates of interest and thus affect investment and the rate of growth. There are also the liquidity aspects of the monetary system. Changes in the supply of money may well affect liquidity "hoards" rather than expenditure on current output.

What the diagram does not show is the twofold relationship between the National Debt and the money supply when the Government is reducing the debt by purchasing it through the open market operations of the central bank. Under these circumstances the cash

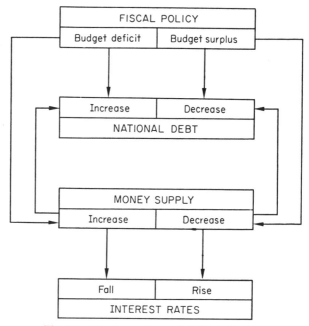

Fig. 7.1   Fiscal, monetary and debt relationships

basis of bank lending is increased and the result is the same as if the Government had purchased the debt with newly printed money. In the opposite case the sale of additional debt transfers money into the hands of the Government. Since money is a highly liquid asset and debt is less liquid, the result of these operations is a change in the liquidity of the assets held by the community. Selling debt tends to lower its price and force up rates of interest. Purchasing debt has the opposite effect. Fig. 7.1 cannot show these relationships which reflect the changing composition of financial assets, nor is the official holding distinguished from the market holding of debt.

Nevertheless, it will be realized that the management of the economy by means of fiscal, monetary and debt policy is a very complicated business. Owing to the existence of expectations, uncertainty, international influences, time lags and the like, it can never be precise.

QUESTIONS ON CHAPTER 7

1. Consider the following possible events:
   (*a*) increase in bank lending;

(*b*) fall in the price of Goverment securities;
(*c*) reduction in the size of the National Debt;
(*d*) increase in official holdings of debt.
Which event would be the most probable result of:
(i) Government purchases of securities through open market operations?
(ii) A budget surplus?
(iii) Pressure on the external value of sterling?
(iv) Increase in bank rate?

2. What do you understand by the following?
(*a*) Monetary Policy;
(*b*) Fiscal Policy;
(*c*) Incomes Policy.

3. Why should Governments wish to influence interest rates?

4. "An increase in the National Debt is inflationary." Discuss.

5. What is the economic significance of the 8 per cent cash ratio of the British banking system?

8 The Government's Revenue and Expenditure

BUDGETS are aids which assist managers and administrators to utilize scarce resources in the economic satisfaction of wants both public and private. The Chancellor of the Exchequer's Budget is similarly an aid to the understanding of how resources have been used in the past year and how the Government plan to use them in the forthcoming year. Strictly speaking a "budget" refers to planned or target values whereas an "account" refers to the values of what has actually materialized during the period under consideration. Budgets are really forecasts whereas accounts are records of actual events. Both the estimates (in the planning sense) and the outturn for the year drawing to a close are, however, included in the United Kingdom Budget[1] which is presented to Parliament at the beginning of each financial year, in April. The financial year, being different from the calendar year, is not the time period to which the National Income and Expenditure Accounts refer, since the latter are aggregated from January to December. Thus some adjustment is necessary before the Exchequer Accounts can be integrated with the National Income Accounts. Fortunately this problem is eased by the production of Exchequer Account figures at monthly and quarterly intervals.

BUDGETARY CONTROL

Budgeting is essential, not only in planning future revenue and expenditure but also in assessing the degree of success or failure arising from variations in policy. Budgetary control is important for assisting with resource allocation and the redistribution of income and wealth. It is also of major importance for the purpose of economic stabilization and growth.

---

[1] *Financial Statement and Budget Report* (H.M.S.O.).

The process of control involves constant checking of the actual accounting results with the budget plan in order to assess whether the latter is being achieved or whether further action is necessary. This may take the form of an adjustment of Government revenue or expenditure or both, possibly through the introduction of a subsidiary budget. A budget may also draw attention to some of the problems as well as suggesting ways of correcting adverse movements. It is not only concerned with flows of income and expenditure (the current budget) but also with changes in the stock of assets (the capital budget).

The Budget which is presented to Parliament is a detailed account of the Government's revenue and expenditure plans for the financial year ahead, along with the outturn figures for the present year. As the year progresses the Government may wish to apply corrective action to the economy through small changes in taxation or expenditure, as mentioned above; and if so mini-budgets may be introduced later in the year. Alternatively, the Chancellor of the Exchequer may vary slightly some of the indirect taxes on commodities in order to regulate the economy. Whatever the direction of the fiscal change, however, it is likely to be accompanied by a complementary change in monetary policy.

Direct Taxation
Direct taxation is collected by the Department of Inland Revenue and includes income-tax, surtax, corporation tax, capital-gains tax, death duties, etc. The Customs and Excise Department collects indirect taxes such as those on commodities, import duties, purchase tax, selective-employment tax, etc.

BUDGET STATEMENT
Since the Budget is a policy instrument for managing the economy the speech by the Chancellor of the Exchequer on Budget Day is essentially a survey of the state of the country from the economic point of view and a forecast of likely developments in the future. The measures introduced in the Budget are later embodied in a Finance Bill which passes through Parliament in the succeeding months, but the *Financial Statement and Budget Report* is published in the form of a White Paper and gives details of the changes in taxation. Another White Paper, *Loans from the National Loans Fund*, gives details of Government lending. This fund is really the Government's capital account since it is concerned with most of the debt finance of the Government through borrowing and lending. On the other hand, the Consolidated Fund is the Government's current account into which revenue from taxation is paid and out of which

current expenditure on supply services is met. Any surplus in the Consolidated Fund is transferred to the National Loans Fund, thus reducing the quantity of Government borrowing. Should there be a deficit, however, in the Consolidated Fund, it is covered by a loan from the National Loans Fund which leads to an increase in borrowing by that amount. Though there are statutory limits to the amounts of money which can be lent to local authorities and public corporations from the National Loans Fund these amounts are not voted annually by Parliament in the same way as the items of current revenue and expenditure which are paid into and out of the Consolidated Fund.

The Financial Statement and Budget Report which is laid before the House of Commons at Budget time is divided into three parts and an annex. The annex shows proposed changes in taxation, its estimated effects, and gives examples of changes in tax paid by single persons and married couples in various income ranges.

Part I gives the economic background to the Budget. It is a review of the past year and forecast of events in the year ahead in terms of the domestic economy and the international economic situation. The review describes the growth of consumers' expenditure, public and private investment, exports, imports and gross national product. The forecasts of these aggregates are compared with their estimated outturns and projections are made for the year ahead.

In Part II of the statement the transactions of the public sector are analysed in terms of their component parts both by economic category of current and capital expenditures and receipts, and then by sector (central government, local authorities, public corporations). Financial transactions are shown in a separate table.

Part III shows transactions of the central government. A summary of Consolidated Fund receipts and issues shows the previous year's Budget estimates compared with their outturns. It also shows the present estimates before and after the Budget changes. The following items are contained in this summary:

CONSOLIDATED FUND

Revenue	*Expenditure*
Taxation	Supply services
Miscellaneous receipts	Consolidated Fund standing services

The surplus (deficit) is transferred to the National Loans Fund. The receipts and expenditure flows are then broken down into various categories. For example, taxation is divided into income-tax, surtax, corporation tax, capital-gains tax, purchase tax, tobacco duties, etc. Expenditure is divided into the various services such as Government and Finance, Commonwealth and Foreign, Agriculture, Education and Science, Defence, etc. For each of these categories there are estimates and outturns, pre-Budget and post-Budget figures.

A summary of National Loans Fund receipts and payments follows, again giving the outturn and Budget changes. The following table shows the main categories:

NATIONAL LOANS FUND

Receipts	*Payments*
Consolidated Fund surplus/deficit	Interest and management of National Debt
Interest receipts and profits from Bank of England Issue Dept.	Loans to public corporations and local authorities

Borrowing

A surplus on this account indicates a net repayment of Government debt. The loans from the National Loans Fund are listed by sector in a separate table as follows:

LOANS FROM NATIONAL LOANS FUND

1. Loans to Nationalized Industries:
    Post Office
    National Coal Board
    Electricity Council
    British Railways Board
    etc.
2. Loans to other Public Corporations:
    New Towns Development Corporations
    Industrial Reorganization Corporation
    etc.
3. Loans to Local Authority Sector:
    Local Authorities
    Harbour Authorities
    etc.
4. Loans to Private Sector:
    Shipbuilding
    Building Societies
    etc.

For each of these categories the past year's estimate and outturn are shown along with the present estimates.

A more detailed statement of these transactions is found in the annual White Paper on Loans from the National Loans Fund which contains reports and comments on the various loans. For each of the nationalized industries the limit of statutory borrowing is compared with actual borrowing, and the relevant statute is quoted.

It is the changes in taxation and expenditure which make the news headlines at Budget time rather than the aggregate values. These changes are set out in the annex to the Financial Statement.

NATIONAL INCOME AND EXPENDITURE BLUE BOOK

A somewhat different presentation may be found in the National Income and Expenditure Blue book. The latest figures for the following items may be found in the current edition:

CURRENT ACCOUNT OF CENTRAL GOVERNMENT

Receipts	*Expenditure*
1. Taxes on income	7. Goods and services
2. Taxes on expenditure	8. Subsidies
3. Dividends, interest and rent	9. Interest on National Debt
4. Gross trading surplus	10. Social security benefits
5. Social security contributions	11. Grants to personal sector
6. Other revenue	12. Grants to local authorities
	13. Grants abroad
	14. Other expenditure

It will be found that taxes on income tend to account for roughly the same proportion of revenue as taxes on expenditure. The largest item on the expenditure side is current expenditure on goods and services. Out of a national income of around £34,000m the Government transfers to itself about £7,000m in taxes on income and about the same amount in taxes on expenditure. Its current expenditure on goods and services is around £5,000m to £6,000m out of a total of about £13,000m. The balancing item is the surplus or deficit on Government current account. This is transferred to the Capital Account in the following manner (see Blue book):

CAPITAL ACCOUNT OF CENTRAL GOVERNMENT

Receipts	*Payments*
(a) Current surplus (a deficit is a negative item)	(f) Gross domestic capital formation
(b) Taxes on capital	(g) Capital grants and transfers
(c) Receipts from transactions in financial assets	(h) Lending to private sector
(d) Receipts from Government borrowing and indebtedness	(i) Lending to public sector
(e) Less increase in gold reserves	(j) Lending to overseas sector

In the current account, item 1 consists of receipts from income-tax and surtax as well as company taxation in the form of corporation tax. Item 2 includes customs and excise duties on beer, wines and spirits, tobacco, hydro-carbon oils, purchase tax, import duties and betting duties. It also includes licence duties and stamp duties. The rent income in item 3 arises from the ownership of property by the Government as well as imputed rent from non-trading property such as Government offices. Various Government departments rent out land and buildings including factories, plant and machinery. Interest is received in respect of loans to the private sector including business firms, loans to public corporations and local authorities and lending to overseas governments. Dividends accrue from the various companies in which the Government holds shares. Item 4 consists of the gross trading surplus from Government trading bodies other than public corporations. As these trading bodies are integrated with the Central Government their cash surpluses are returned to the Exchequer each year. These bodies include the Forestry Commission, the Department of Trade and Industry, the Royal Mint, etc. The Mint is regarded as selling coin to the Government at cost price, this transaction being included in Government expenditure on goods and services. The increase in the face value of new coin is treated as borrowing and features in the capital account of the central Government. Neither item 3 nor item 4 is a transfer item. They both make a direct contribution to the national income. Social-security contributions (item 5) include both flat-rate and graduated contributions to the national health service, pensions, superannuation and unemployment funds. Though selective employment tax is collected with national insurance contributions it is listed separately in the Blue book. Other revenue may include such items as grants from overseas Governments, fees from fines and penalties, and other appropriations-in-aid of Government departments.

On the expenditure side of the current account the first item relates to Government spending on non-trading activities. The main components are wages and salaries of civil servants, purchases of goods and services from the private sector, from public corporations, and from abroad, in respect of defence, social services and economic services. Item 8 is expenditure on subsidies. These are different from grants in that subsidies reduce selling prices (whereas grants are not payments into production accounts). The sectors receiving subsidies include housing, agriculture and transport. Interest on the National Debt (item 9) consists of interest paid by the Government to the non-Government sector. Interest on official holdings is excluded. Item 10, social-security benefits, includes pensions, family allowances, unemployment and sickness benefit, etc. Grants for education form the largest component of item 11. Local authorities receive grants under item 12 which include specific grants as well as general grants. Grants abroad are mainly for economic and military purposes.

The balance on current account represents saving or dissaving and this is carried forward to the capital account, under (a). Taxes on capital, item (b), include death duties, betterment levy and capital gains tax. Under (c) are included the sale of securities and the issue of Government stock in connection with the nationalization of various industries. Government borrowing and net indebtedness (d) includes increases in ways and means advances from the Bank of England to the Government, increases in notes and coin in circulation and in non-marketable debt such as national savings certificates.

95

Also included is the increase in borrowing by means of Treasury bills and securities as well as direct borrowing from overseas governments and the International Monetary Fund. Any increase in gold reserves is deducted because this is shown in the Exchange Equalization Account as corresponding to a reduction in holdings of Government debt. On the payments side of the capital account item (f) consists of fixed capital formation mainly in roads, hospitals and defence establishments and capital formation in stocks and work in progress. Capital grants, item (g), include grants to universities and colleges, capital grants to farmers as well as grants to local authorities and public corporations. Net lending, under (h), includes loans to industry and to private housing associations. Under (i) the loans are to local authorities from the Loans Fund for which the Public Works Loan Board acts as agent, and to public corporations from the National Loans Fund through the various Government departments. Loans are made in this way to such public corporations as the National Coal Board, British Transport Commission, Central Electricity Authority, Gas Council, British Overseas Airways Corporation and the Post Office. Item (j) consists of loans made to various foreign governments under international agreements.

In the Blue book, Government borrowing less any increase in gold reserves is termed the "net balance" and is the extent to which Government expenditure including lending is not covered by taxation and other receipts (both current and capital). The net balance is reflected in item (d) minus the increase in gold and foreign-currency reserves (e). Any repayment of loans to the Government would be included in capital receipts; any repayments by the Government would be included in payments. As changes in international indebtedness and gold reserves are largely the result of external forces it follows that, provided the fiduciary note issue and the issue of coin (by the Bank of England Issue Department) do not change excessively, the balancing item will consist of changes in marketable debt (Treasury bills and Government securities) and changes in the Government's balance at the Bank of England (Banking Department).

The Blue book of the Central Statistical Office presents the accounts of the central Government in a different form from that of Part III of the Chancellor of the Exchequer's Financial Statement. The former accounts are consolidated by eliminating internal transactions within the same sector; they are also rearranged to give a functional presentation which is meaningful in terms of economic aggregates. These principles underlie Part II of the Financial Statement, but the main Exchequer accounts serve to provide Parliament with a system of detailed control since they record transactions of the various departments responsible for the expenditure. These accounts are kept on a cash basis so that they record the flows of cash into and out of the Consolidated Fund. All receipts are paid into this Fund and all payments are made from it. These cash flows are authorized by Parliament through its officer, the Comptroller and Auditor-General. Capital flows are separately accounted for and pass through the National Loans Fund. Payments out of the Exchequer are summarized in the Consolidated Fund Abstract Account. In the Exchequer Weekly Return the totals of receipts and payments are cumulated over the 52 weeks of the financial year. Whereas the Exchequer accounts are audited and serve the purpose of Parliamentary control, the National Income and Expenditure accounts are not audited, being based on estimates of functional economic aggregates. The economic categories are different from those in the Exchequer accounts and they also cut across departmental responsibilities. In the Blue-book presentation, in addition to the usual separation of transactions into current and capital items, a distinction is also made between transactions which are related to the production of goods and services and transfer items, which do not contribute to factor income. The current income and expenditure relating to the National Insurance Fund is shown in a separate account.

In addition to the annual Financial Statement and the National Loans Fund White Paper, there are two more publications which are closely associated with the Budget. These are the Memorandum on Estimates and the White Paper on Preliminary Estimates of National Income and Balance of Payments. All four publications are available around Budget Day.

Part I of the Preliminary Estimates of National Income and Balance of Payments gives the latest figures for the National Income and Expenditure and its components. The tables for G.N.P., Personal Income and Expenditure, Public Sector accounts, etc., are the same as those in the National Income and Expenditure Blue book. In Part II are listed the components of the Balance of Payments. The figures for both parts of the White Paper include not only the calendar year just ended, but also the past five years for comparison.

In the Estimates Memorandum which is presented to Parliament by the Chief Secretary to the Treasury, the supply estimates are summarized and compared with the Budget of the preceding year, class by class, and programme by programme. Later tables analyse expenditure by programme, class and vote, thus making it possible to see the relationship between the Estimates and the annual White Paper on Public Expenditure. There is also a national accounts classification of the Estimates in which it is shown how the expenditure and receipts provided for in the Estimates are recorded in the National Income and Expenditure Blue book. The rest of the Memorandum shows the detailed estimates for the various classes and votes including the vote on account and balance to complete.

Both the Financial Statement and the Estimates Memorandum contain sections in which the presentation of the material is in accordance with the principles on which the National Income and Expenditure Blue book is based, thus making available reliable figures for the public sector which can be integrated in the accounts for the economy as a whole. All the tables in Part II of the Financial Statement and Budget Report are based on national accounting principles.

The purpose of the Exchequer accounts is to enable Parliament to agree to the Government's proposals for raising revenue and for spending it. The detailed form of each estimate allows the Treasury to exercise control over the departments. The division of the estimates into votes and heads allows suitable subjects to be chosen for debate on "supply" days and also enables a detailed examination to be made by the Select Committee on Estimates and the Public Accounts Committee. Parliamentary "supply" procedure votes expenditure and "ways and means" procedure authorizes the issue of money from the Consolidated Fund and also finds ways and means of meeting the expenditure by taxation or by granting additional borrowing powers to the Treasury. Supply procedure votes expenditure for those services which are voted annually by Parliament. Consolidated Fund Services, on the other hand, are fixed by statute and they continue until another statute alters them. Parliamentary financial procedure involves the following steps:

(i) Departmental estimates are forecast to the Treasury for approval some years ahead and are revised at half-yearly intervals before they eventually become the Budget estimates.

(ii) The House of Commons, in supply procedure, deliberates the estimates and grants the votes.

(iii) The House, in ways and means procedure, sanctions the expenditure out of the Consolidated Fund of the required amounts.

(iv) The Appropriation Act at the end of the parliamentary session gives statutory authority to the various amounts of expenditure.

Votes on account are granted by the House towards the end of the financial year to enable the departments to function until the money has been voted for the new financial year.

When expenditure has been approved, the Treasury receive a credit on the Exchequer Account at the Bank of England. As the rate of expenditure does not keep in step with the rate at which tax receipts flow into the Exchequer Account, the Treasury is faced with the problem of raising money at certain times and disposing of it at other times. Excess cash may be used to re-purchase Government debt. A shortage of cash may be relieved by borrowing from other Government departments which have a surplus, or by borrowing from the public by issuing Treasury bills and Government securities. Short-term borrowing also occurs through "ways and means" advances from the Bank of England.

In the Finance Accounts total expenditure on supply services and Consolidated Fund standing services is set against total revenue from taxation and other receipts. The surplus or deficit is taken into account in order to arrive at the net financing requirement. This depends on the amount of loans to industry, etc. The balance is made up of Exchequer borrowing, and includes the issue of both marketable and non-marketable debt as well as ways and means advances from the central bank.

It may be thought that the current account of the Government should be tax-financed and the capital account should be financed by borrowing. This is not so, however, since the solvency of the Government does not depend on its assets (as in the case of a private firm) but on the productivity of the country as a whole and on its taxable capacity. If the distinction between current expenditure financed out of taxation and capital expenditure financed out of borrowing is carried too far one could possibly end up with, say, magnificent college buildings financed from loans, but with a shortage of tax-financed funds for lecturers' salaries and thus insufficient staff to make the new institutions function.

If the central Government accounts are combined with those of local authorities the result is the combined account of public authorities. The combined account for the whole public sector includes central Government, local authorities and public corporations. In preparing these accounts, transactions within each sector are eliminated. In the combined account for the public sector, the revenue from local rates and the trading surplus of public corporations would be included in the receipts side of the current account. The borrowing of local authorities and public corporations would be included on the receipts side of the capital account. From the public sector accounts in the Blue book it will be found that total public expenditure is around £22,000m.

The following is a list of official publications which are available annually and which assist in understanding the financial activities of the public sector and especially the central Government sector:

Available at the beginning of the new financial year:

(a) *Financial Statement and Budget Report*
(b) *Estimates Memorandum*
(c) *Loans from the National Loans Fund*

(d) *Preliminary Estimates of National Income and Balance of Payments*

Available in the autumn:

(e) *National Income and Expenditure* Blue book

Available at the end of the calendar year:

(f) *Public Expenditure* White Paper.

QUESTIONS ON CHAPTER 8

1. Consider the following summary:

EXCHEQUER RECEIPTS AND PAYMENTS

Receipts	£m	*Payments*	£m
Taxation	10,000	Supply services	9,000
Other receipts	2,000	Consolidated Fund	2,000
Revenue	12,000	Expenditure	11,000
Borrowing	2,000	Loans	3,000
Total	14,000	Total	14,000

(a) Is there a deficit or surplus on current account and what is its size?

(b) What do "other receipts" consist of?

(c) What is the difference between supply services and Consolidated Fund payments?

(d) What methods of borrowing are used?

2. What items of revenue are included in the following:

(a) Inland Revenue?

(b) Customs and Excise?

3. What are the advantages and disadvantages of loan finance compared with tax finance of Government expenditure?

9 Taxation

Is our tax system a fair one? Is this or that tax a good one? Questions such as these are difficult to answer for the following reasons:

(a) From the standpoint of equity, benefits should be taken into consideration as well as taxes.

(b) Whether a system of taxes is "fair" or not depends on the criterion used to judge fairness.

(c) An individual tax may be regarded as equitable by one person but unfair by another.

The important thing is that the tax system should be regarded as reasonably fair on average. It should be generally acceptable from the equity viewpoint and individual taxes should not be regarded as flagrantly conflicting with accepted principles of fairness.

Here we shall introduce three groups of criteria which have been expressed at various times by writers on taxation in an attempt to replace arbitrariness by equity based on underlying principles.

1. Adam Smith's Canons of Taxation

In his *Wealth of Nations*, published in 1776, Smith proposed the following four canons or rules:

(i) People should contribute to the expenses of the State in proportion to their revenue or income.

(ii) Taxes should be certain and not arbitrary.

(iii) The times of collection should suit the convenience of the taxpayer.

(iv) Administrative costs should be minimized.

One might consider how far these general principles apply today.

2. The "Ability to Pay" Criterion

This principle was based on the idea that all men are equal before the law and therefore they should be treated equally in matters of taxation. It was realized, however, that economically they were far from equal as they owned varying amounts of property. Thus equality in taxation meant that taxes should take a fixed proportion of the value of land and property. (William the Conqueror's Domesday Survey was probably based on a similar idea.) From the "ability to pay" principle it followed that each person, i.e. head of a household, should contribute in proportion to his wealth. Gradually the principle came to be applied to income rather than property. In any case a tax on land and property would have to be paid out of the income from it, otherwise the wealth would gradually decrease. (This highlights the fact that income is a flow over time whereas property is a stock of wealth in existence at a point in time.)

Some writers have argued that income is no longer a good index of ability to pay taxes. Others regard expenditure as a much better one. These are highly debatable matters.

3. The Benefit Principle

This principle is based on an attempt to see the taxpayer as a recipient of benefits from the State. Thus taxation is the price paid for services rendered just as in the market-place the price paid is a measure of the benefit received—or should be. Applying this principle one could argue that the rich benefit more than the poor from the organization of society and the protection of property; therefore taxation should be in proportion to income. If a tax is paid in order to secure benefits from the State it would seem fitting that individual preferences should fit into the process somewhere. One could argue that preferences are, in fact, taken into account as the adjustment of benefits to taxation comes about through the political process by which, in a democracy, the Government represents the wishes of the people. Do you consider that this explanation is a fairly close approximation to reality? To what extent are the foregoing equity criteria of relevance today?

In the case of direct taxes such as income tax the four canons of Adam Smith seem to have been pretty well realized. It could also be argued that the criterion of "ability to pay" has been more or less satisfied. It is clear, however, that the "benefit principle" may or may not be satisfied. Direct taxes normally tend to take more from those with larger incomes and it is by no means certain that those with larger incomes benefit more than those with smaller incomes. In fact, the opposite will usually be true in a welfare state.

Indirect taxes such as sales taxes are less likely to fulfil Adam

Smith's canons. Nor are they likely to satisfy the "ability to pay" and "benefit" principles.

Both direct and indirect taxation represent a transfer of resources to the Government. The final effects of taxation depend on what the Government does with the money it receives.

REDISTRIBUTION OF INCOME AND WEALTH

One of the objectives of fiscal policy is to secure an equitable distribution of income and wealth. The tax system is the obvious instrument which governments can use in order to achieve this end. Of course, the expenditure side of fiscal policy should not be forgotten—it is becoming an increasingly important means of distributing welfare of various kinds.

Let us assume that the distribution of income before tax approximates to that shown in Fig. 9.1, with the vast majority of income recipients neither very rich nor very poor. What would be the effect on this distribution of each of the following:

(a) a poll-tax which takes a fixed amount of money, each household paying exactly the same amount?

(b) a proportional tax which takes the same proportion of income from everyone?

(c) a progressive tax which takes an increasing proportion of larger incomes?

(d) a regressive tax which takes a decreasing proportion of larger incomes?

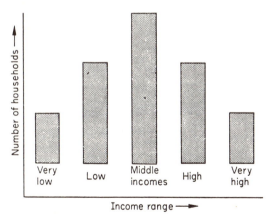

Fig. 9.1 Income distribution before tax

In the diagram the height of each column represents the number of households in each income range from very low to very high. The poll-tax would represent a greater burden on households in the lower income groups than on those with higher incomes. The proportional tax would have a similar effect since, assuming the rate were 20 per cent this would represent a greater burden on a low-income household than on a high-income household.

The progressive tax could radically alter the pattern of income distribution, especially if the rate of progression increased steeply. In this case the right-hand columns in the diagram would be considerably diminished in height. The resulting post-tax pattern would thus show a reduction in the number of households with very high incomes. Similarly, a regressive tax would produce an after-tax pattern with higher columns in the low-income groups.

Progressive Taxation

On what basis can progressive taxation be defended? This question may be found easier to answer if the distribution of income before tax were different from that shown in Fig. 9.1. One could make the left-hand column the highest and let the columns get progressively smaller towards the right. The resulting pre-tax distribution would then be radically altered by a steeply progressive tax.

Consider the pre-tax distribution shown in Fig. 9.2. In order to distribute income from high-income groups to low-income groups it would not only be necessary to have a steeply progressive tax on households in the middle- and higher-income ranges, but also a negative tax or subsidy to households in the lower-income ranges. The combined effect would be to transfer households from the very high and very low ranges to the more central groups of middle incomes.

It can be argued that progressive taxes are fairer than proportional or regressive taxes because an additional £1 of income means more to a poor man than to a rich man. In other words, there is a continuing fall in the marginal satisfaction from additional income. Therefore, in order to produce equality of tax burden, the high-income groups should pay a greater proportion in tax than the lower-income ranges.

Another argument in favour of progressive taxes is based on the fact that our system of taxation contains all kinds of taxes, some of which are necessarily regressive and need to be counterbalanced by progressive ones. In many cases taxes are "passed on" to others via rising prices, lower profits, reduced rates of wage growth, etc. The final resting place or incidence of a tax is not easy to forecast although some taxes are more easily passed on than others. When a new tax is devised the tax base and the tax rate must be clearly defined. For example, a tax on income must define what is meant by "income"— the tax base. Tax rates must also be unambiguous. Some rates are

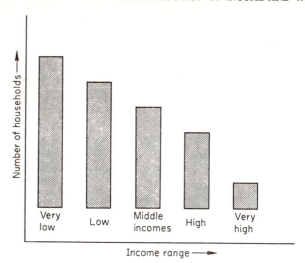

Fig. 9.2 Income distribution before tax

ad valorem rates as in the case of import duties which are a proportion of the price of the imported commodity. Other rates are "specific", e.g. so many pence per litre. How would the Chancellor's revenue be affected by rising import prices if rates were *ad valorem* rather than specific?

The change in the percentage of income taken in tax may be shown diagrammatically (see Fig. 9.3).

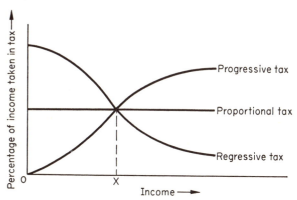

Fig. 9.3 Taxation and income

As pre-tax incomes increase the progressive tax leaves a decreasing percentage of disposable income. It can be seen from the graph that, at income OX, the same percentage is taken in tax under all three types of tax.

105

INDIVIDUAL TAXES

The various taxes which make up the total system of taxation may be examined independently with regard to structure, incidence and probable economic effects. These latter may or may not be the effects which it was intended to produce when the tax was first introduced. One could argue that the chief aim of every tax is to raise revenue for the Exchequer; but it is unlikely that the probable effects of a tax on resource allocation, income distribution, employment and economic stability will be ignored when changes are under consideration.

We shall now examine some particular taxes, starting with those which we call direct taxes and which are assessed separately for each individual or household. Later, we shall look at the structure and effects of certain indirect taxes which are paid as a result of consuming a particular commodity or service.

(i) Income-tax

Although the tax base is income, the rate of tax is applied to taxable income, after various allowances have been deducted. It is possible to have a variety of rates, including a standard rate and a reduced rate on small incomes. The definition of income poses an important problem: it may or may not include transfer payments such as old-age pensions, unemployment benefit, and other social-security payments. Imputed income from the ownership of a dwelling-house may or may not be included. Personal and other allowances, as well as certain expenses, may be deducted before arriving at taxable income to which the rate of tax is applied.

A tax-return guide may be obtained from the local office of the Inland Revenue Department. With the aid of this guide, questions such as the following may be answered:

1. What is the current standard rate of income-tax?
2. Which of the following features are incorporated in the British system of income-tax:
    (a) Reduced rate of tax?
    (b) Earned-income relief?
    (c) Single-person's allowance?
    (d) Dependent-relative allowance?
    (e) Allowance for children aged 11–15 years?
    (f) Expenses incurred in maintaining a dwelling-house?
3. What is included in the definition of income?

Under the Pay As You Earn system (PAYE) income-tax is deducted from weekly wage or monthly salary in accordance with tax tables which indicate the tax to be deducted for each "code number". Each person's code number represents that person's "taxability" after taking into consideration personal circumstances as embodied in the system of allowances. PAYE ensures that each employee is continually in balance with the Inland Revenue Department, cumulative totals of income and tax paid being recorded each week or each month. This is a useful stabilizing factor when inflation or deflation is taking place. Rising or falling incomes will result in rising or falling tax revenues, thus providing an automatic "built-in" contra-cyclical mechanism.

There is a close connection between taxes on income and taxes on capital since a tax on income is a tax on a flow of wealth per annum whilst a tax on capital is a tax on a stock of wealth in existence. Taxes on capital and other forms of property will be discussed later but it is important to note that capital gains, both short-term and long-term, may be treated as income for the purpose of operating a capital-gains tax. These gains may be realized when property (in the form of capital assets) is sold or when it changes hands by gift or inheritance. Short-term gains are those which are realized within a year of acquiring the assets and they are normally treated as ordinary income.

A person who possesses capital will usually expect to receive a return from it in the form of investment income. This may be taxed at a higher rate than income from work or earned income. This tax differential against investment income may be justified on the grounds that the possession of capital is an indication of additional taxable capacity. On the other hand it can be said that the tax discriminates against those who save, since much investment income arises from savings out of earned income.

In the British system of income-tax and surtax progression is achieved by the rapid rise in surtax rates as well as by the use of a system of allowances and deductions. In order to see the possible effects of a progressive rate of tax it is necessary to distinguish between the marginal rate of tax and the average rate of tax. The marginal rate is the actual rate of tax charged on additional income. The average or effective rate of tax takes into account the various allowances, reduced rates, etc. For example, consider the tax on a person whose income, all earned, is £2,000 per annum. Assume the post-tax income is £1,300 and the tax of £700 is made up as follows:

the first £500 of income pays no tax;
the next £500 pays £100 tax—a rate of 20 per cent;
the next £500 pays £200 tax—a rate of 40 per cent;
the final £500 pays £400 tax—a rate of 80 per cent.

These are the marginal rates of tax and account for the steps in Fig. 9.4. The average rates can be calculated as follows:

On an income of £1,000 the tax is £100 or 10 per cent;

On an income of £1,500 the tax is £300 or 20 per cent;
On an income of £2,000 the tax is £700 or 35 per cent.

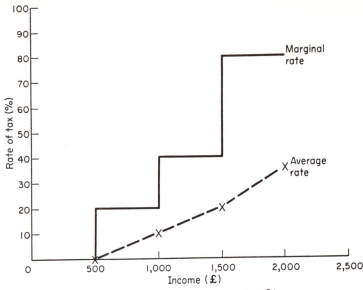

Fig. 9.4   Marginal and average rates of tax

It can be seen from Fig. 9.4 that the higher the marginal rate the more it pulls up the average. The difference between the marginal and the average rate is an important factor to be taken into account when considering the effect of income taxation on the supply of effort. Although it is true that the amount of post-tax income is only one of many motivating forces, the gain in equity from high marginal rates of tax should be counterbalanced by the possible loss in work effort. It can be argued that the status symbol of a high pre-tax income plus fringe benefits provides an important incentive to effort, but nevertheless the disincentive effect of taxation could be reduced by keeping average and marginal rates as close together as possible.

It might be expected that people would increase their work effort if both average and marginal tax rates were lowered. This may well be true for some people; others may respond by leaving their work effort unchanged or even reducing it. In any case many workers are not in a position to adjust their supply of effort—this being governed by current agreements between employers and trade unions or by custom. On the other hand, at the top end of the income scale high surtax rates may encourage newly trained professional people to take up employment in those countries where marginal and average tax rates are relatively low.

Up to now we have been concerned with personal income-tax as it affects an individual or household. Income, however, may also be earned by a business firm in the form of profit and so we must look briefly at the taxation of corporate income.

(ii) Corporation Tax

A company earns income in the form of profit which is the difference between total revenue from sales and total costs of production. This profit provides additional taxable capacity for the Exchequer, because, by treating companies as entities separate from their shareholders, it is possible to subject them to company taxation in the form of corporation tax. This is assessed on taxable profit after deducting the various allowances which normally include such items as debenture interest, allowances for depreciation and obsolescence of capital in the form of plant and machinery, and special grants and allowances to encourage investment, especially in regions where the economic rate of development is lower than the average for the country as a whole. It is possible to have a system of company taxation which taxes dividends (distributed profits) at a higher rate than profits which are retained in the company in order to provide funds for expansion. The reasoning behind such a system is that by this means private investment in new capital projects will be encouraged. Unfortunately there is no guarantee that this is what actually happens. In practice, companies may be encouraged to use the funds for the purchase of additional short-term investments, thus adding to the liquidity of the economy.

Under the more usual system of corporation tax, business profit is taxed at a rate of, say, 30 or 40 per cent and that part which is "ploughed back" into the business pays no further tax. The part which is distributed to shareholders, however, will be subject to income-tax and surtax at the appropriate rates since this part of the firm's profit becomes personal income for the shareholders.

Let us assume that a company, after deducting the various allowances, has a taxable profit of £12,000 and that it decides to retain £2,000 and to distribute the rest to its shareholders. Corporation tax at, say, 40 per cent will provide £4,800 for the Exchequer. Thus shareholders will receive not £10,000 but only £5,200 and from this amount the Exchequer will receive a further revenue in the form of income-tax and surtax.

There are many problems connected with the taxation of companies. In the first place, sole proprietors and partnerships normally have their business profits subjected to income-tax and surtax as private individuals. Secondly the accounting period of a company may not coincide with the fiscal period for corporation-tax purposes. Thirdly there are problems connected with the treatment of the depreciation of fixed assets which may be "written off" either on the basis of historical cost or on that of replacement cost. In times of inflation depreciation based on historical cost will not produce sufficient funds for the replacement of the asset when it is worn out. Fourthly there is the question of companies with branches abroad which are subject to foreign company taxation. The offsetting of foreign tax may be a matter for international agreement. Finally there is the matter of the differential treatment of distributed and undistributed profit. In the example quoted above, any profit which is distributed pays income-tax as well as corporation tax.

Some companies make losses from time to time and the tax provisions may allow losses to be offset against profits in a later accounting period. A multi-product firm may be at an advantage over a firm which is in one line of production only, for the former company may have a number of lines which are unprofitable so that losses may be offset against profits on other lines. Clearly this will enable the multi-product firm to take the risks entailed in the introduction of new lines. Where a firm is operating under fully competitive conditions the forces of competition will tend to move that firm into a marginal position where it earns only standard or normal profits. If corporation tax were based on this definition of profit the marginal firm would find it difficult to remain in business. On the other hand, where firms are operating under partially competitive conditions or under conditions of monopoly, and thus earning monopoly profits, a proportional tax would be unlikely to alter the most profitable price and output positions. Consider the case shown in Fig. 9.5 where cost and price are measured vertically and output horizontally:

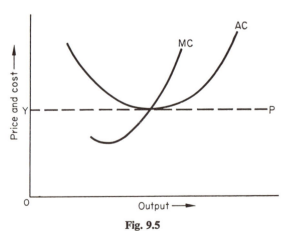

Fig. 9.5

AC and *MC* are the average and marginal cost curves of a firm

110

operating under fully competitive conditions, and the standard or normal profit necessary to keep this firm in business is included in these curves. A proportional tax on the firm's profits can be absorbed by the firm provided that market price is greater than OY (shown by the broken line). If the price is equal to OY then the firm is a marginal one and it will be able to continue in business on condition that standard or normal profit is tax free and tax is paid only on profit over and above the standard. Under monopoly and partially competitive conditions there will usually be sufficient profit being earned to absorb the tax. A possible result of the tax in conditions such as these is a smaller amount of investment in capital projects than would have been the case in a non-tax situation.

(iii) Taxes on Property

It can be said that taxes on property are necessary from the viewpoint of the redistribution of wealth. Do you consider that land, capital and other physical assets form a suitable tax base? Taxes on property certainly fill gaps in the general taxation system and taxes on land have an extremely long history. A more recent innovation is the tax on gains arising from the development of land. It is held that these gains are, in the main, provided by the community itself through development programmes which include the planning of new roads, new shopping areas and new towns. A special tax or "betterment levy" may be imposed on the property owner who benefits from a rise in the value of his land when he decides to sell it. A betterment levy may take a fixed proportion of the increase in value (say 40 per cent) or it may be progressive. It may be argued that this tax is unfair to owners of very small amounts of land especially if the tax is a proportional one.

The word "levy" is usually reserved for "once for all" tax payments and at various times a capital levy has been imposed on all owners of capital above a certain minimum value. Of course the valuation of existing assets gives rise to many problems. For example, what is the most appropriate rate of interest to use in order to arrive at the present value of an asset? By discounting back the future stream of receipts to which an asset gives rise, an estimate of its present value may be obtained.

Though it may be said that a capital levy is non-recurring it may be hard to convince people that the levy will not be repeated at some time in the future and this may have a deterrent effect on saving.

Reference has already been made to the capital-gains tax since capital gains may be treated as income. The tax is payable when the assets are disposed of. Losses are normally allowable as offsets to the tax. It has been said that the tax is a deterrent to saving.

If a person buys antique furniture for £1,000 and later decides to sell it for £1,500 then his gain of £500 may be subject to tax, depending on the length of time he owned the asset before disposing of it, and also depending on whether the asset falls into one of the categories of assets attracting tax. (Note that owner-occupied houses are generally exempt.)

Capital gains may be divided into short-term and long-term gains. The buying and selling of securities on the Stock Exchange is one of the main activities giving rise to short-term gains.

It is also worth mentioning that when certain assets are transferred from one owner to another these transactions attract tax in the form of stamp duties.

Estate duty is normally charged on estates when the owner dies. This property tax is usually highly progressive with an exemption limit at the lower end of the scale. In times of inflation, estates tend to move from one value range to the next higher range, thus attracting taxes at a higher rate.

Apart from utilizing taxable capacity, the taxation of property passing at death is based on the desire to secure a more equitable distribution of wealth. It is often said that inherited capital and gifts are a form of potential expenditure to the recipient and that this additional taxable capacity, if utilized, is less likely to be a deterrent to saving than a tax on investment income. Of course, those families which suffer a succession of deaths at short intervals are liable to heavy estate duties.

Another form of property taxation is the local rate. Rates are local taxes on property values and will be discussed in Chapter 11.

(iv) Taxes on Expenditure

It was shown in Chapter 4 that national expenditure is simply another way of looking at national income. Does it follow that it is immaterial whether the Government draws its tax revenue from the income flow of the economy or from the expenditure stream? From the individual's point of view, it can be argued that a given amount taken in income-tax will leave him with more "welfare" than the same amount taken in commodity taxation. Although the usual analysis is in terms of "indifference curves" a simplified version is shown in Fig. 9.6. Since income is measured vertically and commodities horizontally an income OC will purchase OZ of commodities and, similarly, incomes of OB and OA will purchase OY and OX of commodities respectively. Thus lines such as CZ, BY, AX have slopes representing the "price" of commodities. A tax on commodities will raise this price; for example the line CX represents a higher price after the imposition of a commodity tax, since income OC will now purchase only an amount OX of commodities.

The commodity tax drives a wedge into the price mechanism, so

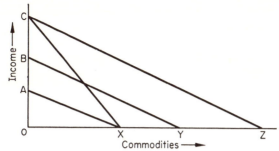

Fig. 9.6 Income tax and commodity tax

that not only are prices raised but in many cases output is reduced, thus distorting the pattern of production which consumers would have preferred. Indirect taxation of this kind might result in a commodity revenue to the Exchequer equivalent to *YZ* and a reduction in output represented by *XY*. One could argue therefore that an income-tax equal to *BC* would result in the same commodity revenue to the Exchequer and this tax would be preferred by tax-payers since it would not interfere with commodity prices and consumer choice.

Taxes on selected commodities such as tobacco, alcohol and petrol (hydro-carbon oils) are important revenue raisers. The effect on price and output of a tax on a selected commodity will depend on the elasticities of demand and supply. It may be thought that a tax on a commodity would raise the price by the same amount as the tax but this is not normally the case. Under competitive conditions a tax on a commodity can be regarded as moving the supply curve to the left since the amounts which would have been supplied at various prices in the pre-tax situation will now be supplied at price plus tax. This is shown in Fig. 9.7, where *AS* is the pre-tax supply curve and *BT* is the supply curve after the imposition of a tax equal to *AB*.

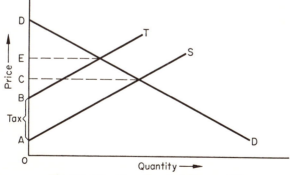

Fig. 9.7 Taxation of a selected commodity

113

It can be seen from the diagram that the pre-tax equilibrium price was OC and the equilibrium price after tax is OE; thus the price has risen by CE which is less than the tax, AB. Note, however, that at the new equilibrium price less of the commodity is being produced and consumed.

If the selected commodities are those with inelastic demand and supply curves then consumption will not fall very much and there will be little tendency for productive factors to move out of the industry. On the other hand if these curves are highly elastic the tax will be likely to result in a considerable fall in demand and output. Imagine a tax being imposed on a commodity which had a number of close substitutes, all tax-free. Consumers would tend to prefer the substitutes and the demand for the taxed commodity would fall off causing the revenue expectations of the Exchequer to be unfulfilled. This is shown in Fig. 9.8, where AS is the pre-tax supply curve and PD is the demand curve. BT is the supply curve after the tax has been imposed.

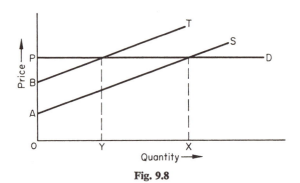

Fig. 9.8

It might be expected that a tax equal to AB would produce a revenue equal to BA times OX, since OX is the amount being sold at price OP. Unfortunately, after imposing the tax, sales fall to OY so that the actual revenue is only BA times OY.

A selective tax on the output of a particular commodity is a constant addition to variable costs. These costs vary as output changes, but if they are constant over a certain range the increase in price will tend to be equal to the tax. On the other hand if these costs are rising, as is the case under competitive conditions, the increase in price is less than the tax, since output will fall with a consequent decline in costs.

In the case of a firm operating under conditions of partial competition or monopoly, the most profitable output will occur where marginal cost and marginal revenue coincide. The effect of the tax will depend on the way the marginal cost and revenue curves change as output changes. Fig 9.9 shows the average and marginal revenue and cost curves for a monopolist. Under the conditions shown on the diagram monopoly profit is given by *AB* times output *OX*.

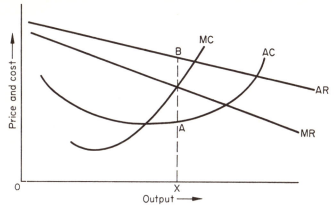

Fig. 9.9 Revenue and cost curves of a monopolist

A tax on the commodity which raises the cost curves will tend to reduce output when marginal cost moves to the left of *B*. It may be said that, since monopoly output is less than the output which would have been produced under competitive conditions, there would be a further loss of welfare if the tax were so high that output was restricted further.

Purchase Tax A more general tax on a group of commodities may be imposed at a variety of rates. Purchase tax is a tax of this nature and luxuries may be taxed at the highest rate whilst necessities are taxed at a much lower rate. Other groups of commodities may be taxed at intermediate rates. Though these rates can be varied quickly in response to a change in general economic conditions (a short-term regulating device) there are problems connected with the classification of commodities into their respective groups. Since purchase tax is normally an *ad valorem* tax, rising prices will increase the yield in times of inflation.

The following is an example of the classification into groups for purchase tax:

I Motor-vehicles and motor-cycles
II Radio, gramophones, television
III Clothing and footwear
IV Hardware and household goods
V Medicines and cosmetics

115

VI Confectionery
VII Furniture

Sales Tax   A more general type of expenditure tax is the sales tax which may be imposed on all sales of commodities at the same *ad valorem* rate. It may be expected that a general tax of this nature would raise prices in the same proportion; but in reality this would not be the case since elasticities of demand and supply are usually different for each commodity produced. A general, *ad-valorem* sales tax of 25 per cent is illustrated in Fig. 9.10.

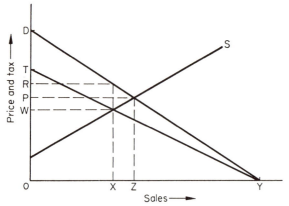

Fig. 9.10   Sales tax

The supply curve is *S* and the demand curve is *DY*. Under competitive conditions the pre-tax price is *OP* with sales *OZ*. *DT* is 25 per cent of *OD* and *YT* represents the demand curve net of tax, since at each sale 25 per cent of the price is taken in tax. The post-tax price is *OR* and sales *OX*. Out of a total revenue of *OR* times *OX* the tax absorbs *WR* times *OX*. A general sales tax is not only regressive but a tax of, say, 25 per cent would tend to be absorbed more easily by the consumers of highly-priced luxury goods than by the consumers of low-priced necessities. The tax is not levied on the intermediate stages of production but is imposed when commodities and services are sold to the consumer.

Turnover Taxes   Turnover taxes are a species of taxes on expenditure since turnover is another way of looking at spending. The problem with turnover taxes is that they are usually of the "cascade" type. This means that there is a tax on the turnover of the manufacturer and the wholesaler, as well as a tax on the retailer's turnover.

This duplication of points of impact adds to the burden of administrative costs and is an important incentive to vertical integration with a consequent growth of monopolies and partial monopolies. Turnover can best be interpreted to mean total revenue, which is the revenue from the sales of output. This revenue includes production costs, profit, investment and depreciation. It would be expected, therefore, that all these components would be affected by the tax. Consider Fig. 9.11, where revenue and costs are measured vertically and production and sales horizontally (it is assumed there is no addition to stocks).

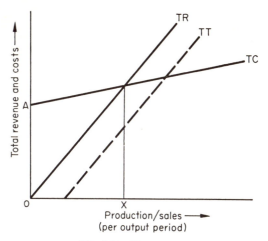

Fig. 9.11 Turnover tax

TC and *TR* show the relation of total costs and total revenue to output. At output *OX* the firm breaks even and profits are made at all outputs greater than *OX*. The turnover tax will shift the total-revenue line into a position such as the broken line *TT*, thus moving the break-even point to the right. It would pay this firm to amalgamate with another firm in order to avoid the tax.

Value-added Tax   The value-added tax (V.A.T.) is a refinement of the cascade form of turnover tax in that the tax is on the value of the net addition to output of a business, usually in the form of a proportional tax. The tax is paid in full by the final consumer as it is included in the price paid for the commodity or service. The tax is collected by the Government in stages, however, as the commodity passes through the economy from one business firm to another. Although a firm is taxed on its output, it subtracts from its tax liability the tax which has already been paid on its various inputs. This information would be shown on the invoices it receives from the firms supplying raw materials, partly-finished goods, etc. At all stages of production there is both a tax liability and a tax credit, but when the final consumer makes his purchase there is a tax liability but no corresponding credit. In the case of exports, however, the turnover is not subject to tax. Exports, therefore, are supplied at prices based on their costs. This places them in a more competitive position than is the case when taxes such as corporation tax are levied, as these tend to increase costs. The value-added tax is a basic tax in the countries of the European Economic Community. When an indirect tax is levied on a small range of commodities only, such as fuel oil, tobacco and alcoholic drink, the rate of tax is normally fairly high in order to produce the revenue required. A value-added tax falls on the whole range of goods and services, apart from those which are specifically exempted, and therefore the rate of tax is usually fairly low, say 5 per cent on most products and 20 per cent on certain luxury products.

Though the tax is applied to capital goods as well as to consumer goods, the purchaser of capital goods deducts the tax already paid, when working out his own tax liability. Thus it is the services of capital goods and not the equipment itself which bears tax. The final output includes the contributions made by capital and it is these which bear tax and not capital accumulation as such. Assume that a manufacturing company purchases the following inputs:

	Price (£)
Raw materials	1,000
Power and light	100
Plastic bags	50
	1,150

If V.A.T. is 10 per cent, and the purchase price of these inputs does not include tax, they will be invoiced at £1,150 plus £115 tax, making a total of £1,265. If the manufacturer now adds £1,000 to the value of the goods by processing them his tax liability is found as follows:

	£	
Total cost of inputs	1,265	of which tax is £115
Cost less tax	1,150	
Value added	1,000	
Selling price (net of tax)	2,150	
Tax at 10%	215	
Selling price (including tax)	2,365	
Tax liability of manufacturer	215	less 115, i.e. £100.

Thus the manufacturer's tax liability is 10 per cent of the value added (manpower costs and profits).

It can be said that such a tax increases business efficiency since it is not assessed on profits alone as is the case with a corporation tax. This argument rests on the assumption that greater profits represent greater efficiency, but this need not necessarily follow. It is true that the V.A.T. does not discriminate between distributed and undistributed profits; it is also true that it can encourage exports, especially if it replaces a tax which has tended to raise export prices through its effect on costs.

Personal Expenditure Tax A personal expenditure tax may take the form of a proportional tax on personal expenditure or, alternatively, a progressive one. The basis of such a tax is taxable expenditure, consisting of total annual receipts less savings and investments. Receipts include money borrowed and sales of investments. Selected expenditure can be exempted from such a tax.

The main advantages of a tax on personal expenditure are as follows:

1. Expenditure is a better measure of taxable capacity than income, since the problems connected with the differential treatment of investment and work income, and of the assessment of capital gains, do not arise.

2. A rate of progression can be applied to an expenditure tax as well as to an income-tax.

3. An expenditure tax would exempt savings from taxation and would not discriminate against risk-bearing. It might even reduce the disincentive effects of taxation on the supply of effort.

4. It is claimed that an expenditure tax would give the Government a flexible mechanism for controlling the economy.

On the other hand a tax on expenditure has been criticized on grounds of administrative expense and of difficulty in arriving at a proper definition of personal expenditure.

(v) Taxes on Business Costs

These taxes usually take the form of taxes on factor inputs such as labour, raw materials, industrial land, business property and transport.

A fixed tax in the form of an annual licence duty will increase the fixed costs of the business. Marginal cost and marginal revenue will be unchanged. The firm will include the tax under its "overheads" but if the tax were significantly large it could turn a firm's profit into a loss. In Fig. 9.11 the effect of the tax would be to raise the TC line parallel to itself thus increasing the distance OA.

A selective employment tax may be imposed as a specific amount per worker employed. A tax of this kind may differentiate between manufacturing industries and service industries, between male and female workers, between full-time and part-time workers, etc. Since the tax makes the use of manpower more costly, one would expect to see a tendency to substitute labour-saving equipment where possible.

Since capital-intensive methods tend to be more productive than labour-intensive methods, an increase in productivity may be expected from such a tax. An example of this might be a reduction in the number of counter staff in retailing and the expansion of self-service.

Taxes on imports of raw materials may take the form of specific or *ad valorem* custom duties or a general surcharge on imports of both raw materials and finished goods. The problem is complicated by the fact that many of these commodities can be produced in the home country; but the effect of the taxation of imports on output and price depends on various elasticities. The relevant ones are the elasticities of demand and supply, not only of the imported commodity, but also of competing home-produced commodities. As well as price elasticities of demand, income elasticities must be taken into account in estimating the full effect.

ECONOMIC EFFECTS OF TAXATION

Taxation is only one component in the overall scheme of fiscal management of the economy. Nevertheless it is useful to highlight the various objectives of taxation. (Negative taxes or subsidies may be regarded as falling on the expenditure side of the Government accounts rather than on the revenue side.)

The main aims of taxation are as follows:

1. Revenue-raising for the provision of public goods and services. This involves a switch of resources from the private sector to the public sector of the economy.

2. Redistribution of income and wealth. This assumes that there is some socially desirable pattern of distribution which it is hoped to achieve.

3. To encourage or discourage selected outputs or the use of selected inputs. This is achieved by means of the incentive–disincentive system of taxes and subsidies.

4. Closely related to 3 is the objective of securing a satisfactory balance-of-payments position.

5. The maintenance of a full-employment level of activity, both on a regional basis and in the economy as a whole. Coupled with this is the objective of planned expansion of the economy over time.

Individual taxes may be considered in the light of the objectives listed above, and many of them will be found to be extremely efficient in achieving the desired ends. On the other hand, a tax which helps to secure one of the objectives may well work against the achievement of others and in many cases there may be side effects which feed back into the economic system. It is instructive to consider the effect of a particular tax on such economic activities as savings, consumption, work effort, investment and exporting. A change in the structure of a tax will normally alter its economic effects. For example, a narrowing of the gap between marginal and average rates of income-tax will tend to lessen the disincentive effect on work effort. The substitution of goods with low price elasticities of demand for those with high elasticities will lessen the distortion of the pricing system when taxes are imposed on selected commodities.

During a period of inflation the burden of taxation will change even if tax rates remain the same. Most changes, however, are deliberate policy changes in order to achieve some specific objective. For example, a capital-gains tax may be the result of an endeavour to widen the concept of income. An increase in the tobacco tax may reflect a desire to curtail the habit of smoking. The encouragement of a particular industry such as the shipbuilding industry may be expressed in high investment allowances. Selective employment tax may be refunded to certain industries in order to increase the mobility of labour. Exports may be stimulated by means of a rebate of value-added tax.

Whatever the economic effects of a particular tax or of the system of taxation as a whole, it is of paramount importance that taxation should be regarded as equitable. People in similar economic positions expect to be treated equally and people in dissimilar positions should be treated according to some generally accepted standard of fairness —which may not, however, mean the same thing at different times. An equitable system of taxation is one of the prices we have to pay for social stability.

QUESTIONS ON CHAPTER 9

Questions 1 to 5 refer to the following events:
  (i) a rise in the prices of currently-produced commodities;
 (ii) an increase in Government revenue;
(iii) substitution of labour for capital in production;
 (iv) an increase in the level of savings;
  (v) a more equitable distribution of income.

1. Which events are likely to occur as a result of an increase in the level of corporation tax?
  (a) (i) only?
  (b) (ii) only?
  (c) (iii) and (iv)?
  (d) (i) and (ii)?
  (e) (v) only?

2. Which events would probably be the outcome of a reduction in the standard rate of income-tax?
  (a) (i), (ii) and (iii)?

(b) (ii), (iv) and (v)?
(c) (ii) and (iv)?
(d) (ii) and (iii)?
(e) (ii), (iii) and (iv)?

3. Which events would be likely to occur as a result of an increase in the level of capital-gains tax?

(a) (i) and (ii)?
(b) (iv) only?
(c) (v) only?
(d) (ii) and (iv)?
(e) (iii) only?

4. If there was an increase in purchase tax which of the following outcomes would be most likely?

(a) (ii) and (v)?
(b) (iii) and (v)?
(c) (ii) and (iv)?
(d) (iv) and (v)?
(e) (i) and (ii)?

5. Which events would be the probable outcomes of a reduction in selective employment tax?

(a) (v) only?
(b) (ii) and (iii)?
(c) (iii) only?
(d) (iv) only?
(e) (i) and (v)?

6. Consider the possible economic effects of an annual tax on personal wealth. The base of the tax would be total accumulated wealth and the rate would be proportional.

7. What would be the likely economic effects of substituting an earnings-related contribution for a flat-rate social-security contribution? Assume the tax is shared equally by employers and employees.

8. "Equity in taxation means treating equals equally and unequals fairly." Discuss.

9. Should husband and wife be treated as one unit for tax purposes or should they be taxed separately?

10. Complete the blanks in the following table from the latest figures.

TAX RECEIPTS

£ million

Taxes on income
Taxes on capital
Local rates
Taxes on expenditure
Social-security contributions
Total
(See National Income and Expenditure Blue-
book, H.M.S.O.)

11. What are the main characteristics and objectives of a value-added tax?

10   Public Expenditure

PUBLIC expenditure embraces all the public-sector spending including that of the central Government, local authorities and public corporations with the exception of the operating-account expenditure of these last. Total public expenditure thus consists of the current and capital expenditure of the central Government and local authorities as well as the capital expenditure of public corporations. Although the current expenditure of the public corporations is excluded, where they are subsidized on current account the amount of the subsidy is included.

There are various ways of classifying public expenditure. For example it may be classified by economic category, by function, or by the responsible administrative department. One possible grouping is as follows:

    (i) Defence and overseas aid;
    (ii) Social services;
    (iii) Economic services;
    (iv) Administration;
    (v) National Debt interest;
    (vi) Miscellaneous.

Aspects of Government policy are reflected in this grouping. For instance, item (i) reflects the Government's foreign policy. Item (ii) reflects policy on education, health and welfare. Economic services (iii) include subsidies to farmers under the Government's agricultural policy as well as expenditure on roads and railways in connection with transport policy, and assistance to private industry especially in relation to development-area policy. Item (v) is influenced by the size of the budget surplus or deficit; by changes in the composition of the debt (short-term debt relative to long-term) and by movements in rates of interest.

Another useful classification differentiates between current and capital expenditure and further subdivides these into:

(*a*) purchases of goods and services;

(*b*) transfers in cash or in kind.

A transfer, being a single movement of purchasing power from the Government to persons, businesses or other governments, does not involve a movement of goods and services in return.

Public expenditure is concerned partly with the preservation of the community through the provision of defence, law and order, etc., and partly with the improvement of the community's welfare through the provision of public goods and services which assist in the satisfaction of collective wants. The maintenance of economic welfare results from public expenditure which is incurred as part of the Government's stabilization policy.

The functional classification of public expenditure in the Blue book depends on the division of expenditure into Votes each concerned with a particular purpose. This classification includes:

Military defence	Roads and public lighting
Transport and communication	Housing
Libraries, museums and arts	Police
Parliament and law courts	Prisons
Education	Fire service
National Health Service	Finance and tax collection

There are many other functional categories in the classification and for each of these the expenditure is divided into:

(i) Current expenditure on goods and services;

(ii) Gross domestic fixed capital formation;

(iii) Increase in value of stocks;

(iv) Current grants;

(v) Capital grants;

(vi) Subsidies;

(vii) Loans.

These economic categories are further subdivided by sector where applicable. For example, the gross domestic fixed-capital formation of local authorities is distinguished from that of public corporations. Also current grants to the private sector are distinguished from current grants abroad.

From the Blue-book figures it can be seen that the bulk of public expenditure consists of current expenditure on goods and services. The second place, in order of importance, is shared by capital formation and current grants to personal sector.

The Treasury analysis of public expenditure (to be found at the end of the Blue book) shows expenditure in terms of the programmes of the various Government departments. Thus it is closely related to parliamentary policy. For example, expenditure on roads may be subdivided into:

Major roads
Other roads
Lighting, car parks, etc.
Departmental administration.

Thus, in certain cases the Treasury analysis is more detailed, in others less detailed. Current and capital expenditure are not shown separately except for the nationalized industries.

PUBLIC EXPENDITURE PROGRAMME

In an economy with a large and important public sector the problem of planning the various programmes calls for a fairly long-term view of the future. All long-term plans, however, have to be integrated in the annual Budget plan which is concerned chiefly with short-term economic stability of employment and prices. The normal procedure which is followed by the Government departments is based on the recommendations of the Plowden Committee on the Control of Public Expenditure (Cmnd. 1432). A regular survey of public expenditure as a whole is presented to Parliament by the Chancellor of the Exchequer in the form of a White Paper towards the end of each calendar year. The prospect for public expenditure is given not only for the current financial year but also for each successive year over the next four years. Thus the survey for 1971–72 gives expenditure estimates as far as 1975–76 and each succeeding survey rolls the figures forward a year. Expenditure for year 1 is the current programme. Expenditures for years 2 and 3 are more or less committed and form the basis for departmental plans. Expenditures for years 4 and 5 are provisional. Year 3 is regarded as the final opportunity for making substantial changes in expenditure programmes. In year 2 only marginal changes are normally possible. Year 3 is thus a time of re-examination and modification of the plans which have been rolling forward.

Not all expenditure plans follow exactly this pattern. In the case of defence it is usual to plan ahead over a period of, say, ten years. On the other hand, educational building programmes may be geared to a "starts" programme in the second year of a four-year pattern.

In the White Paper on Public Expenditure the following three categories of transaction are distinguished:

(i) use of resources: including current and capital expenditure on goods and services and grants abroad;

(ii) transfer payments: including social-security benefits, subsidies and interest on the National Debt;

(iii) assets: including net purchases of land, buildings and financial assets.

Against this expenditure is listed projected receipts based on probable trends but there is no certainty about the receipts side of the table as tax rates, etc., may be changed at short notice in order to regulate the economy. The layout of expenditure and receipts follows the pattern set out below:

PUBLIC EXPENDITURE AND RECEIPTS

Receipts	*Expenditure*
(A) Resources:	
Charges	Purchase of resources for current capital purposes
	Less charges = Net expenditure
(B) Transfers, taxation, etc:	
Taxes	Grants and subsidies
Contributions	Debt interest (domestic)
Other receipts	
(C) Assets:	
Taxes on capital and miscellaneous borrowing	Net purchase of land, existing buildings and financial assets

The amounts of the various items are given in £m at current prices for the present year's outturn and also for each of the succeeding three years in the form of estimates. Since the White Paper is published around December the financial year will have ended in the previous March and the outturn figures will be available. The estimates for the financial year in which the White Paper is published and for the succeeding years are based on existing policies and decisions. The balance between the receipts and expenditure sides shows the net financial requirement of the public sector, but the necessity for borrowing in any given year may not be what is indicated. This follows from the fact that the outturns of the programmes may be different from the estimates and the general level of prices may change. More important is the fact that the level of taxation is not actually decided until Budget Day and may be adjusted at any time in order to regulate the economy.

It will be noticed that there are three main groups of items in the above layout. These are (A) Resources, (B) Transfers and (C) Assets.

Resources

Resources are used up in the production of the current national output. Thus, all expenditure on goods and services by the public sector, whether for current use or as gross investment, falls within

126

this category since it represents a direct claim on the country's available resources. Examples are the purchase of educational materials, the salaries of civil servants and the provision of new Government offices. Net payments abroad are also included here since they represent a use of resources through unrequited exports. The charges and sales revenue on the receipts side is regarded as offsetting to some extent the current expenditure on goods and services. Receipts include charges for school meals and welfare foods. These charges are subtracted from expenditure to arrive at the net balance of expenditure on resources.

Transfer Payments

Transfers (B) form the second main group. On the expenditure side is shown public-sector spending on grants, subsidies and debt interest, all of which represent a less direct call on resources than (A) since they have a "feedback" effect on receipts. Part of these payments return to the Government in the form of taxation, contributions, etc. These receipts are shown on the left-hand side. If they were not set against expenditure the use of resources would be different from that shown. Another important point to notice is that grants and subsidies may not give rise to immediate spending. Some part may be saved, or may be used to purchase existing assets such as land or stocks and shares, with consequent effects on prices and liquidity. Thus, because of feedback effects on taxation and effects on saving, the relation between changes in transfer payments and changes in aggregate demand may be difficult to assess. It has been estimated that about one-fifth of extra expenditure on goods and services by the private sector flows back to the Government via indirect taxation. An increase in transfer payments in the form of National Debt interest would only result in part of the increase being spent on goods and services since a stream of income-tax and surtax payments would be generated. Some proportion of the remainder would probably be saved. Assuming that direct taxation and saving accounted for just over one-third of the increase in interest payments, indirect taxation would account for about one-fifth of what was left for spending on goods and services. Thus the effect on aggregate demand is much less than the original transfer payment.

Some transfer payments in the form of social-security benefits, such as sickness and unemployment benefits, are free of tax. Others, such as widows' and retirement benefits, are taxable. In both cases, however, there will be some feedback to the Exchequer through purchase tax and other taxes on expenditure.

Under an earnings-related social-security scheme, both contributions and benefits are on an earnings-related rather than a flat-rate basis, with the result that, as incomes increase, the percentage contributions to the Social Insurance Fund and Superannuation Fund bring in a greater total of receipts. Public-sector expenditure is raised by the increase in the total of earnings-related benefits.

Assets

The third group of public-sector transactions is Assets (C), in which receipts from taxation of assets, such as estate duty and capital-gains tax are set against expenditure by the public sector on the purchase of land, company securities, etc., as well as net lending to the private sector. The main effect of these transactions is to affect the liquidity position of the economy, although there may be some effect on aggregate demand, after a time-lag.

Since all the amounts of expenditure and income are expressed at constant prices (i.e. base-year prices) this enables a comparison to be made between one year and the next and between one item and another, without having to bother about changes in the general level of prices. This procedure, however, underestimates the importance of public-sector expenditure when productivity is rising steadily over the years. Consequently an allowance is made for the "relative price effect" so that the proportion of the gross national product taken by public-sector expenditure is correctly expressed. If this were not done, the gradual rise in the productivity of labour in the private sector which is reflected in rising real wages, and which leads to a rise in real wages in the public sector in order to keep the balance, would not be taken into account. After all, every rise in private-sector productivity means that the opportunity cost of using scarce resources in the public sector also rises, since they can produce more in the private sector than formerly.

Other Classifications

In addition to the summary classification into resources, transfers and assets, there are other important classifications of public expenditure. One of these is by groups of programmes as follows:

Programme Group	Outturn year n £m	Estimate year n+1 £m	Estimate year n+2 £m	Estimate year n+3 £m
1. Defence	..	..	..	..
2. Commerce and Industry	..	..	..	..
3. Environmental Services	..	..	..	..
4. Social Services etc.	..	..	..	..

This layout is also given in much greater detail by dividing the groups into subgroups. For example, Social Services may be divided into Education, Health and Welfare and Social Security. A similar presentation of expenditure is made by classifying the figures by spending authority and distinguishing between current and capital expenditure. The spending authorities are the central Government, local authorities and public corporations.

Finally the White Paper classifies expenditure and receipts by programme and by type of transaction for each of the survey years. For each programme such as Defence, Transport, Housing, etc., receipts and payments are shown for each of the three groups—resources, transfers and assets. The net balance for each group is shown along with the total balance of resources, transfers and assets. This total is different from the total of public expenditure as the latter shows net expenditure on resources, plus transfer payments, plus purchase of assets.

Individual Programmes

The general prospects for public expenditure are dealt with in Part 1 of the White Paper on Public Expenditure. In Part 2 the individual programmes are examined in more detail. Certain programmes may be commented on as follows:

(i) *Technological Services*   This expenditure programme is divided into activities for which financial management is flexible and those major projects which are long-term commitments. Industrial research establishments expenditure is included. They provide a service for industry as well as for the public sector. An example is provided by the work of the National Research Development Council. Also included is expenditure on civil-aircraft projects, contributions to space programmes and assistance to specific industries.

(ii) *Other Assistance to Industry*   In this programme is included expenditure on employment services, the youth-employment service and payments from the Redundancy Fund. The promotion of local employment takes place through loans and grants to business firms providing employment in the development areas, and the cost of building new factories and industrial estates. The Industrial Re-organization Corporation* promotes industrial reorganization where there are economic benefits to be obtained from it. The loan capital on which it pays interest comes from the National Loans Fund, but it also receives Government finance in the form of capital on which it pays a dividend. The Corporation supports industrial mergers where these are likely to result in important economies. Private industry also benefits from investment grants which have as their aim the increase in productive investment especially in development areas.

(iii) *Agriculture, Fisheries and Forestry*   This programme consists

---

* Phased out in 1971.

129

of Government support for agriculture, fisheries and both private and State forestry. Over three-quarters of the expenditure is on agricultural support which depends on guaranteed prices, agreed at the annual price reviews, and on fluctuations in market prices. Other payments include grants for farm modernization and development.

(iv) *Transport* The programme covers support to the nationalized industries, especially British Rail. Expenditure on roads and public lighting is included in a separate programme. Port investment accounts for a substantial part of the total expenditure as also does the rebate of duty on motor-bus fuel and grants to road-passenger transport organizations. Other expenditures are associated with the operation of civil airports.

(v) *Housing* This expenditure programme is concerned with increasing the stock of houses by encouraging new building in both the public and private sectors and with improvement in the existing stock through modernization. Capital expenditure on new housing by local authorities is largely financed by loans as is also much of the expenditure on replacement and mortgages to housing associations, etc. Housing subsidies to local authorities take account of the level of interest rates they have to pay on loans to finance new building. This applies to interest rates in excess of 4 per cent. Local authorities' funds are also subsidized by the central Government in order to lower the level of council-house rents.

(vi) *Law and Order* Current and capital expenditure relate to police, prisons, probation service, child care, fire service, and the Law Courts. Expenditure on legal aid, Parliament and the Privy Council and general elections is also included. Forecasts of expenditure have to take account of social factors such as the growth of crime, the annual number of fires, etc.

(vii) *Education* The size of this programme is related to the increase in the pupil and student populations. Expenditure is incurred in respect of schools, colleges, universities, youth service, school-meals service, libraries and administration. Local authorities are the main spending agents and a large proportion of the expenditure is on wages and salaries of teachers. Total expenditure on this programme is running at nearly 8 per cent of G.N.P.

(viii) *Health and Welfare* The bulk of this programme relates to current and capital expenditure on hospitals but also included are family-practitioner services, community health and welfare services, other central services and grants, welfare foods and administration. Much of the capital expenditure is concerned with the replacement and modernization of hospitals. A high proportion of current expenditure is on wages and salaries of hospital staff.

(ix) *Social Security* Expenditure on this programme is affected by demographic factors such as the age structure of the population, sickness and mortality rates and customary age of retirement.

Non-contributory schemes such as war pensions are financed completely from general taxation. Contributory schemes, on the other hand, are partly flat-rate schemes and partly earnings-related. Included in expenditure are pensions and superannuation, sickness benefit, unemployment benefits, industrial-injuries payments and family allowances.

(x) *Capital Expenditure by Nationalized Industries* This programme of public investment is divided between the various public corporations. The bulk of the expenditure on fixed assets is accounted for by the Post Office, Electricity Council and Boards and Gas Council and Boards. The rest of this expenditure is undertaken by the following:

National Bus Company
National Freight Corporation
British Steel Corporation
British Railways Board
British Transport Docks Board
British Overseas Airways Corporation
British European Airways
British Airports Authority
British Waterways Board

plus the British Broadcasting Corporation, Independent Television Authority and other miscellaneous public corporations.

The figures for capital expenditure are gross figures and the major proportion of this expenditure is for replacement of assets. Other individual programmes of public expenditure are given for defence, overseas aid, research councils, roads and public lighting, local environmental services, arts, financial administration, common and miscellaneous services.

EFFECT OF CHANGES IN GOVERNMENT EXPENDITURE

The presentation of public expenditure in the White Paper differentiates between transfer payments and expenditure on resources for providing goods and services. It also makes the necessary distinction between current and capital expenditure and, by expressing the figures at constant prices, the expenditure of one year can be related to that of another. Thus changes in expenditure programmes should reflect changing Government policy based on underlying changes in population and other social and political factors.

Under full employment the opportunity cost of additional public expenditure is reflected in the resources which the private sector has to relinquish. Similarly the opportunity cost of additional private resource-use is reflected in the resources which could have been used in the public sector. It may be argued that some interpretation of "taxable capacity" sets an upper limit to public expenditure at full employment, but as national income expands the acceptable lower limit of public expenditure tends to rise with it. Thus the choice between private- and public-sector resource-use occurs within a framework of growth in available resources. Analysis of this allocation problem involves the theory of the political process and the effect of the voting system on the size and distribution of public expenditure, and its division between the various levels of government. The division of spending between these levels may be considerably affected by technical progress which leads to large-scale organization in the public-administration sector as well as in the private sector. If total public expenditure is, say, 50 per cent of G.N.P. the actual share taken by the public sector is less than this, since transfers and subsidies do not form part of the national income. On the other hand, transfers and subsidies need to be financed and there are as many different implications for the economy as there are different methods of finance.

Theoretically, the community would secure maximum welfare from a spending programme if the marginal benefit were equal to the marginal cost. This is indicated by expenditure OX in the following diagram:

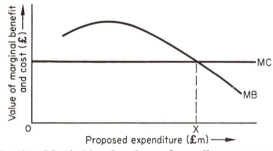

Fig. 10.1 Marginal benefit and cost of expenditure programme

The marginal benefit is shown by the MB line which is assumed to fall eventually as expenditure on the service increases. MC is the marginal cost which is parallel to the horizontal axis since total expenditure is measured along it and is assumed to be proportional to the amount of the service provided.

This emphasizes the fact that, in real life, expenditure decisions are rarely concerned with "all or none" but with "a little more or less". Public expenditure is related to various objectives of policy and in many cases there are alternative forms of expenditure which can be used to secure each objective. It is one of the proper functions of government to produce the required results with the most economic expenditure of scarce resources.

In order to take account of all the ways in which its decisions affect the community the Government makes use of cost–benefit analysis where possible. This analysis values the costs and benefits of the proposal under consideration and compares it with alternative proposals, thus aiding the Government in its decision-making. For example, in comparing the costs and benefits of nuclear and coal-fired power stations one of the important factors to be taken into account is unemployment. There is no cost to the community in employing manpower which would otherwise remain idle. Other factors which are included in cost–benefit valuations are saving in time, pollution, amenities and accidents. One of the benefits from supporting agriculture is the amenity benefit of a rural countryside. It may not be possible to value this exactly, nevertheless a shadow price may be imputed for the purpose of the analysis. The Management Accounting Unit at the Treasury co-ordinates the work in cost–benefit analysis being done in the various public-sector organizations. It decides on the test discount rate which the nationalized industries use in making their investment proposals. A valuation has been agreed for both working time and leisure time so that changes in them can be taken into account when cost–benefit analysis is applied to transport problems.

QUESTIONS ON CHAPTER 10

1. From the latest White Paper on Public Expenditure extract the outturn figures and compare them with the estimates of future expenditure for the following categories:
   (a) net expenditure on resources;
   (b) transfer payments;
   (c) net purchase of land and existing assets;
   (d) current expenditure of central government;
   (e) current expenditure of local authorities;
   (f) capital expenditure of public corporations;
   (g) interest on the National Debt.

Express (a) as a proportion of G.N.P. and explain the significance of this ratio.

2. What economic and social factors influence the expenditures classified under (*b*) and (*g*) in question 1?

3. "The amount and rate of increase of public expenditure is determined not by what the community thinks is desirable but by what it thinks is an acceptable burden of taxation." Discuss.

4. What is the economic significance for Government spending of the growth of population and changes in its age distribution?

5. What determines the ratio of (*d*) to (*e*) in question 1?

11 Revenue and Expenditure of Local Government

IT has been stated that the public sector consists of central Government, public corporations and local authorities. If public corporations are not included we have the public-authorities sector composed of central Government and local authorities. In the present chapter, however, we are concerned only with the revenue and expenditure of that level of government represented by local authorities, but it must be remembered that this term embraces a variety of administrations both large and small.

RELATION BETWEEN CENTRAL AND LOCAL GOVERNMENT

Though local authorities act as spending authorities for many public-sector programmes it would not be true to say that they are merely spending agents for the central Government. They not only raise a large amount of revenue by local taxation in the form of rates but they also make their own expenditure decisions in connection with the provision of a wide variety of local services. Local authorities in the United Kingdom are responsible for about 30 per cent of total public expenditure. Well over a third of their current expenditure is on education. The tendency towards large-scale reorganization in local government results in larger administrative areas with the bulk of local-authority expenditure becoming the responsibility of a smaller number of authorities.

The central Government exerts a closer control over local authorities' capital expenditure than over their current expenditure. When local authorities wish to finance a project by borrowing, for example, the central Government must first sanction the loan and, in the case of major programmes such as school-building and housing, specific approval is required for the start of the project. One of the advantages of local control over the provision of services is that it gives freedom to the local authority to experiment with new ideas and new systems. Against this, however, must be set the diversity in the quality of service offered by different authorities, unless the central Government lays down uniform minimum standards.

Difficult problems arise in regions where, owing to the steady development of industrial and residential areas, present-day economic boundaries no longer coincide with actual legal boundaries. This happens when people in the higher-income groups move outside the city boundaries in order to secure better living conditions. Even industry may follow this trend when, for example, in order to bring about a reduction in costs, factories are built outside the city near a motorway or an airport. Congestion, pollution and deteriorating housing are external diseconomies leading to increasing expenditure by the local authority. Unfortunately the revenue from rates generally fails to keep pace with the increased spending, so that more and more reliance has to be placed on financial assistance from the central Government in the form of grants. Also the growth of a suburban population beyond the city boundary may place a heavy burden on an existing small local authority. Thus it is possible that the optimum size of administrative unit is much larger than that which occurs in practice. Economies of large-scale organization may be available in such spheres as water supply, sewage and refuse disposal, local road and transport systems and education.

It may be said that local government is the most appropriate spending authority when the services to be provided require local knowledge and understanding of local conditions. Equally it can be argued that local branches of central Government departments would be more effective in providing nation-wide services of a uniform standard.

There are obvious social benefits to be gained from uniform standards of service and there are economic benefits to be gained from large-scale organization. Where local authorities differ to a large extent in wealth and income, uniformity of service over the whole country may not be achieved. With regard to the benefits of large-scale organization, the securing of these advantages may require local government to be organized on a regional basis.

In the National Income and Expenditure Blue book the local authority sector includes, as well as the ordinary administrative authorities such as county and borough councils, local river and harbour authorities, water and drainage boards and similar local administrative organizations. Most of the figures are derived from the annual *Local Government Financial Statistics*. The current account of local authorities is made up as follows:

LOCAL AUTHORITIES—CURRENT ACCOUNT

Receipts	*Expenditure*
(i) Rates	(v) Purchase of goods and services
(ii) Grants	(vi) Housing subsidies
(*a*) General	(vii) Current grants to personal sector
(*b*) Specific	(viii) Debt interest
(iii) Rent and interest	
(iv) Gross trading surplus	

Balance = current surplus/deficit before providing for depreciation, etc.

RATES

About 80 per cent of local authorities' current income comes from rates and grants. Grants, which the local authorities receive from the central Government, account for a greater part of current revenue than rates, but the latter are an important and independent source of income. The local rate is a tax on the annual value of land and buildings in the local authority's area, and is under the direct control of the authority. Since its yield is not subject to undue fluctuation from year to year the local rate provides a steady source of revenue. The valuation of land and property which is the basis of local rates is carried out by the Valuation Department of the Inland Revenue in an endeavour to obtain fairly uniform assessments over the whole country. The local authority then decides on the rate to be paid on each £1 of rateable value. For example a local authority may levy a rate of 80p in the £ made up as follows:

For local authority purposes	55·50p
For police	12·50p
For river authorities	1·00p
For higher authority purposes	11·00p
	80·00p

In this example, part of total revenue is paid over to a higher or regional authority for services provided. These may include such services as administration of justice and the probation service, ambulance and fire service, town planning and research, etc.

The rate may be varied according to the type of use made of the land and property. For example, domestic use may be charged less than business use. Agricultural use may be charged at very low rates or not charged at all. Rates may be varied in order to benefit certain industries or certain geographical regions such as the development areas.

One of the criticisms of the local rate is that it is regressive against income, but this is a general criticism of taxes on expenditure. Provided that local rates are not taking an excessive proportion of

137

income the regression may be compensated by the income-redistribution policy of the central Government.

The rising demands of social services, especially education, health and housing have meant a growing burden on local rates, although this has been reduced from time to time by transferring certain services from the local-authority sector to the central Government. Hospitals, for example, were transferred to the National Health Service. Apart from local rates, Parliament reserves the right to all taxes; thus it is inevitable that grants should be given by the Exchequer to assist in the financing of local-authority services.

Local Income-tax

It has been said that the reliance on central Government grants may be reduced by the introduction of a system of local income-tax. It has also been stated that a local income-tax has certain advantages over local rates as a means of raising revenue for local authorities. It is true that a local income-tax could be made progressive with income, whereas the local rate is regressive; but against this must be set the disadvantage of relinquishing some of the central Government's control over progressive taxation as this is an instrument not only for redistributing income, but also for stabilizing the economy; an objective which requires central management. Also, a local income-tax which differs from one local authority to the next may well encourage a movement of population away from the highly-taxed areas. It is also highly probable that a local income-tax would cost more to administer than a local rate.

If a flat-rate local income-tax were introduced at, say, 6p in the £, without any progression or allowances, there would be little advantage over the system of local rates from the equity point of view. On the other hand, if the rate were made progressive, the richer areas would tend to produce much more revenue than the poorer ones and the system of central Government grants would need to make due allowance for the variations in local-authority income which would arise. If business firms were included in the system of local income-tax the further problem would arise of the allocation of business income to different local authority areas when firms operate in more than one area. Though it may be possible to devise a local income-tax which would reduce the disadvantages to a minimum it would seem that the balance of advantage lies in retaining the income-tax system within the central Government sector. This is true, also, of a local sales tax, since stabilization policy requires the central Government to exert control over a variety of flexible fiscal instruments.

GRANTS

The central Government grant is the usual instrument for supplementing the revenue which local authorities receive from local rates. Grants are divided into those which are allocated to a specific service and those which are not so allocated but which can be put to general use.

The specific services for which grants have been paid include roads and public lighting, police, administration of justice, child care, education, etc. These grants, however, form only a small proportion of the total grant payment by the central Government. The general grant accounts for most of the total. One of the policies underlying the system of general grants is that of maintaining the independence of local authorities in the detailed allocation of their revenue between the various services they provide; another is to provide adequate financial assistance for the poorer authorities. The amount of rate-support grant is determined by the central Government on the basis of estimates of local authorities' revenue in the forthcoming year. In determining grant payments it is usual to apply a formula in which the main factor is the difference between the total revenue raised by a 1p rate in the local authority's area and the average for the country as a whole. Other factors which may be included are the number of children under a certain age, the percentage of unemployment in the area and the degree of poverty. For example, the total amount of rate-support grant paid to all local authorities may be determined by subtracting total specific grants in aid of revenue expenditure from aggregate Exchequer grants (which may be fixed at, say, 60 per cent of estimated expenditure). Consider the following example:

	£m
Estimated local authorities' expenditure	4,000
Aggregate Exchequer grant (at 60 per cent)	2,400
Specific grants	400
Thus, rate-support grant (aggregate) =	2,000

The aggregate rate-support grant for any year is divided into three parts or elements. The domestic element provides relief for domestic ratepayers as against business ratepayers. The resources element brings those authorities whose resources are below the national average (in terms of the product of a penny rate) up to that average. The needs element takes into account such items as population, children under school age, old-age pensioners, etc. Supplementary payments take account of educational provision and roads.

In contrast to the arrangements governing general grants, those which determine specific grants normally take account of the total cost of the service, and the central Government grant is a percentage of this. Alternatively the grant may be of the unit type which gives a specific amount of money per unit of service provided.

The main objective of allocated grants is to encourage local authorities to provide some specific service. They are often conditional upon the provision of a certain minimum standard and they may vary according to the authority's financial resources.

Once a minimum standard has been achieved with the help of a specific grant it may be possible for Parliament to prescribe the minimum standard and make it legal, with the result that specific grants may be converted into general ones.

RENT AND INTEREST

The next item on the receipts side of the local authorities' current account is rent and interest. Rent arises from the ownership of dwelling houses and other property such as schools to which a rent is imputed. Receipts of interest accrue from local-authority loans to individuals for house purchase and from the investment of funds. Rent and interest together account for under 20 per cent of local-authority income.

Gross trading surplus is shown before providing for depreciation and accounts for only a small proportion of receipts. The chief activities reflected in this item are water supply, harbours, docks and airports, passenger transport, markets and cemeteries.

The relative importance of the different sources of local-authority revenue can be judged from the figures given in the National Income and Expenditure Blue book. Where a considerable change has taken place in the figures for one of the categories of receipts this may usually be explained by a change in the policy of the central Government.

EXPENDITURE

With regard to current expenditure by local authorities on goods and services, the following programmes are included:

(a) *Social Services:*
   Education
   Health
   Welfare
   Child care

(b) *Environmental Services:*
   Sewerage and refuse disposal
   Public health
   Land drainage and coast protection
   Parks, pleasure grounds, etc.

Libraries, museums and arts
Roads and public lighting

(c) *Other Services:*

Administration of justice
Police
Fire service, etc.

The provision of housing is treated separately in connection with housing subsidies. The bulk of local-government current expenditure is on communal services and especially on the social services. Education is by far the most important item, accounting for over 50 per cent of total current expenditure, with a constantly rising trend. Environmental services include not only essential services such as sewerage and public-health services which are basic to the standard of welfare of the community, but also a number of services designed to improve the local environment such as sports facilities and parks.

Housing subsidies are included on the expenditure side since they represent the deficit on housing services which is financed by the central Government. The deficit arises because the amount raised in rents is less than the current expenditure on repairs, loan charges, etc., and the subsidy is similar to a reduced rent from the tenant's viewpoint. New house building, which is financed out of borrowing, appears in the local authorities' capital account.

Current grants to the personal sector are mainly in the form of students' grants for fees and maintenance allowance. The cost of legal aid is also included in this category.

The surplus or deficit on local authorities' current account is transferred to capital account as shown below under item (a):

LOCAL AUTHORITIES' CAPITAL ACCOUNT

Receipts	*Payments*
(a) Current surplus (or deficit)	(e) Gross domestic fixed capital formation in:
(b) Capital grants	Housing
(c) Borrowing from central Government	Environmental services
(d) Other borrowing	Social services
	Trading services
	Other services
	(f) Capital grants to personal sector
	(g) Net lending for house purchase.

(The surplus/deficit on this account shows the change in cash balances and liquidity.)

Capital grants are payments by the central Government towards capital expenditure on specific services, the main ones being roads, environmental services, education and housing. Borrowing from the central Government relates to advances from the Local Loans Fund through the agency of the Public Works Loan Board and from various Government departments. Other borrowing refers to both long-term borrowing by means of the issue of securities, and short-term borrowing of a temporary nature.

On the payments side, capital formation in fixed assets is most important in the case of housing, education, roads and environmental services. Education is of growing importance. New housing is financed by borrowing. Central-Government subsidies to local authorities help to defray the interest charges on the loans. Capital grants to the personal sector are mainly for the improvement of existing houses and local authorities also make mortgage loans to residents for the purpose of house purchase.

Government policy towards housing is partly reflected in the housing subsidies received by local authorities towards their loan charges on new housing and conversion programmes. Part of the subsidy enables a reduced rent to be charged to tenants of local-authority houses. Another side of housing policy is concerned with the control of rents in the private sector. As with all capital goods, houses need to be maintained and eventually replaced or rebuilt. Rent is the price paid by the tenant-occupier to the owner of a property in exchange for the use of it over a certain period of time. Thus, from the owner's point of view, rent is an income from investing in property and, if the return from the investment is insufficient to cover maintenance and other charges as well as bringing an appropriate return on the investment, then other forms of investment may prove more attractive to investors. If it is decided to place an upper limit on rents by some form of rent control existing property owners will have little inducement to maintain and improve their property owing to the relatively small return on it. Also when rents are fixed below their market price not only is the supply of rented accommodation diminished, but also the demand is increased, with greater pressure on local authorities to supply additional rented accommodation.

Government interference with the market mechanism in housing is justified on the grounds of equity since a dwelling-house is a necessity so that the demand tends to be inelastic, and consequently any increase in rates or maintenance cost tends to be passed on in the form of higher rents. The supply of houses is probably less than it would be if they were not subject to tax. The system of local rates probably tends to divert some resources from the taxed product. Another reason for Government concern over housing is to be found in the effect of poor housing on the health of the community. It is as desirable to secure a minimum acceptable standard of housing as it is to secure minimum standards in the environmental services of sewerage and refuse disposal. Thus, Government interference with the free play of market forces may be justified on welfare grounds. The following diagram illustrates a policy of rent control:

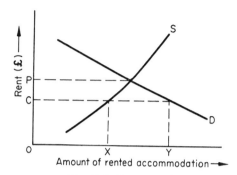

Fig. 11.1   Rent control

D is the demand curve for rented accommodation. The supply curve of rented accommodation (*S*) tends to be inelastic since annual additions of new houses and flats make only a minimal difference to the existing stock. The free-market rent *OP* is derived from the inter-section of these curves. If a controlled rent of *OC* is imposed there will tend to be a pressure of demand equal to *XY* which the public sector may try to eliminate by making additional rented accommodation available.

Population growth and the development of the central areas of towns tend to raise ground rents and site values, thus exerting an upward pressure on the rents of houses and flats. The opportunity cost of living in these areas rises owing to the competition for the available space from developers who wish to extend the provision of shops and offices in response to demand. Thus, new sites in the suburbs will be found for housing schemes and even industry may move away from the centre to areas of lower cost. Rising incomes also exert an upward pressure on the demand for housing and, since the building industry is fairly labour-intensive, a steady demand is matched by an upward trend in costs, reinforced by rising site values. This results in the building of a substantial number of residences per acre of ground.

Apart from housing subsidies and State assistance to housing associations, local authorities provide capital grants for improvements and mortgage loans for house purchase in the private sector. An important influence on building is the policy of town planning which aims at the overall development of services in an area.

The upward trend in local authorities' provision of housing, education, roads and environmental services accounts for most of the increase in capital expenditure which is financed by borrowing either from the Public Works Loan Board or through the issue of stock to the general public. Interest rates on loans from the Public Works Loan Board are varied from time to time and these changes affect the amount of money which is borrowed from other sources. Chief of these is the issue of bonds such as "yearling" bonds. Local authorities also borrow fairly heavily from the money market in advance of their rate income. This borrowing takes the form of temporary loans from merchant banks, other banks and financial institutions, and from time to time includes the raising of money abroad.

QUESTIONS ON CHAPTER 11

1. Consider the economic problems involved in the provision of education by local authorities and discuss any alternative method of organizing the provision of this service.

2. From the Blue book on National Income and Expenditure extract the figures for the various categories of revenue from the current account of local authorities. Discuss the probable causes of any changes that have taken place in the relative importance of the various sources of revenue.

3. Using the Blue-book figures for local authorities' current expenditure comment on any relative changes that have taken place, mentioning probable reasons for them.

4. What are the main items of local authorities' receipts and expenditure on capital account?

5. "The local rate is a measure of the services provided by the local authority." Discuss.

6. Explain the distinction between general grants and specific grants with reference to their objectives? What are the main types of grant in use today?

7. What are the advantages and disadvantages of local income-taxes compared with present-day methods of financing the expenditure of local authorities?

8. How far is it true to say that local authorities are simply the spending agents of central Government?

12 Government Economic Policy

STATE economic policy is executed at various levels of Government, central and local. It is important for the economy as a whole that the revenue and expenditure plans of local authorities as well as the investment plans of public corporations should be integrated with the programmes of the central Government to give a complete picture of the effect of the public sector on the economy. It is not easy to assess the net effect of a change in Government expenditure on the level and rate of growth of national income since any change reacts upon other aggregates such as capital investment, imports and exports, taxation and productivity.

Nevertheless Government economic policy can be said to be concerned with the level and rate of growth of national income, its distribution between the various classes in the community, and its composition in the sense of the provision of public and private goods and services. Within this general framework are many sub-policies such as the encouragement or discouragement of a particular line of production or the modification of the conditions of production and distribution. Current policy towards agriculture or to the manufacture of dangerous drugs is an example of the former. Monopoly policy and legislation about restrictive practices is an example of the latter.

The instruments by which Government policy is achieved include not only fiscal and monetary controls but also more specific controls such as those which have been exercised over incomes and prices or over regional economic development.

MONOPOLY

Consider the control by the State of monopolistic practices in the private sector of the economy. Monopolistic organizations originate in a number of ways. Single-firm monopolies arise through takeovers and mergers, the control of a single source of supply, the advantages of large-scale organization, etc. Monopolies have also developed through price and quantity agreements between different firms producing similar products.

It cannot automatically be assumed that monopoly always leads to an inefficient use of resources and high prices for the consumer. Where there are obvious economies of large-scale production through, for example, computerized processes or mass-production methods, it is possible that a monopoly will be more efficient than a number of competing firms. This is likely to be the case when expenditure on research is an important element in the long-term production programme.

United Kingdom policy is to judge each monopoly on its merits. The consumer is generally in a weak position when the monopolized commodity is a necessity since there will be no alternatives to which he can turn, whereas under competitive conditions the consumer will have a selection of lines from which to choose. These circumstances place a monopolist in the position of being able to restrict output and force up the price owing to the fact that the demand is inelastic. The Government may, therefore, deem it to be desirable to control the monopoly in the public interest. The Monopolies Commission is empowered to investigate the activities of single-firm monopolies and to examine the economic consequences of mergers. The existence of the exercise of monopoly power may be revealed by exceptionally high profits, the charging of discriminatory prices or the restriction of entry to the industry of would-be rivals. Agreements between firms for the reduction of output or the maintenance of a common pricing policy are dealt with through the mechanism of the Registrar of Restrictive Practices and the Restrictive Practices Court. In order that an agreement be allowed to continue it must be shown to be in the public interest since it is generally accepted that monopolistic agreements tend to lead to a wasteful use of resources through the under-production of the monopolized product.

STATE CONTROL OF ECONOMIC ACTIVITY

State policy towards monopoly is an example of an extension of the legal framework of the State to the activities of production and distribution. This framework has always provided the basic rules under which production, distribution and exchange take place. Examples are mercantile law, industrial and trade-union legislation, and so on.

Within this broad legal framework the Government influences the economy through the activities of the whole public sector consisting of central Government departments, local authorities and public corporations. The latter exert considerable influence on the economy through the activities of the nationalized industries especially in the form of capital investment. They also affect employment and productivity directly. Improvements in efficiency are partly the result of the application of management tools such as output budgeting, cost—benefit analysis, discounted-cash-flow investment analysis, etc. Increased productivity is also one of the aims of the Industrial Training Boards whose main function is to further the provision of sufficient suitable manpower for each major industry.

BALANCE OF PAYMENTS

The operations of the public sector react on resource allocation in the private sector of the economy. One of the major objectives of Government economic policy is the maintenance of the economy on a path of stable growth at an optimum level of activity. The methods used to secure stability are both fiscal and monetary. The latter operate within the institutional framework of the banking system which is as involved with international monetary flows as with domestic ones. Thus Government policy must take account of changes in the balance of payments as well as of the effect of its own policy on the international economic situation. Costs and prices are related to the rate of wage increases and also to the country's competitive position abroad. When a balance-of-payments deficit continues without sign of improvement the Government may resort to devaluation in an attempt to correct the adverse balance. On the other hand the external value of the currency may come under pressure if there is widespread belief that some other country is about to revalue its currency. When a country has a strong balance-of-payments position this is usually reflected in a steady demand for its currency. The opposite is also true, so that when the United Kingdom balance of payments is running a deficit there will be pressure on the Exchange Equalization Account which is charged with the task of maintaining the external value of the currency. There may also be increased borrowing from the International Monetary Fund and other central banks to meet a situation of this kind. A high bank rate is a monetary measure which is closely associated with the foregoing. The balance of payments is also affected by movements of short- and long-term capital. It is not only relatively high interest rates which attract foreign capital and affect the external balance, but also there is the balance-of-payments effect of low interest rates attracting borrowers. An example of the latter is the raising of funds on West European capital markets by United Kingdom local authorities and nationalized industries.

With regard to the domestic economy, a high bank rate is usually coupled with measures of credit restriction whilst a low bank rate is associated with credit expansion. Restriction includes the setting of upper limits to lending by the banks and finance houses. Also included in a policy of credit restraint is the system of special deposits by which the Bank of England requires the commercial banks to place a proportion of their deposits in a special account at the central bank. Though these deposits may earn a small amount of interest they cannot be included in the bankers' cash ratios or in their liquid-assets ratios. Special deposits, along with bank rate and adjustments to the supply of money, give the Government control over the amount of bank lending and liquidity.

For the restraint of consumer spending, as an element in effective demand, the Government relies heavily on fiscal measures in the form of increased taxation. The Budget is also directed at influencing the level of total investment demand, not only through tax changes but also through changes in public-sector expenditure. When Budget expectations are not fully realized, Government policy may require the introduction of supplementary budgets. Economic policy may also be directed to the productivity aspect of the economy, but this policy is likely to take the form of measures to reduce the number of industrial disputes and the associated loss of output. This may be achieved by modifying the legal framework of industry rather than by using financial instruments.

Price Mechanism

Since the price mechanism is regarded as a reasonably efficient method of allocating resources it might be asked why the Government should interfere in its operation. It is obvious that on grounds of equity an acceptable distribution of income and wealth requires the use of fiscal policy for its achievement because the distribution which would otherwise result would not be acceptable. Apart from this, however, there is the general problem of economic stability, a sphere in which the Government has a special responsibility for the maintenance of full employment and the curbing of inflation.

On other grounds too the Government may positively modify the resource allocation which would be brought about by the price mechanism. This mechanism, when working under perfect competition, influences the allocation of resources through the profitability associated with the optimum output of each business at the established market price. Efficiency in production then depends on that level of output being produced at the least possible cost. An efficient allocation of resources results from this process since the price paid for a product equals its marginal cost of production. The greater the element of monopoly, however, the weaker this process tends to be;

consequently the Government concerns itself with an appropriate monopoly policy which, if successful, will tend to reduce the gap between marginal cost and price.

The working of the price system in the private sector of the economy does not take account of social benefits and costs which are the result of external economies and diseconomies. Only those costs and benefits which are of direct concern to the business firm are included in the profitability calculations of management. This profitability in the financial or commercial sense is different from the balancing of costs and benefits in the wider social sense. The latter would not normally be taken into account; therefore Government intervention in the form of taxes or subsidies may be required. External economies and diseconomies are of considerable importance in the public sector where they influence the expenditure programmes not only of the public corporations but of central and local Government as well.

It must not be assumed that the price mechanism, because it has certain shortcomings, is not a useful and powerful instrument for allocating resources. When social costs and benefits are not taken into account a system of taxes and subsidies may compensate for this deficiency. As well as in the markets for goods and services, the price mechanism is an important instrument for maintaining equilibrium in the markets for manpower, capital and in foreign trade since wages, interest rates and exchange rates are prices of a particular kind. The maintenance of equilibrium in the economy as a whole has its counterparts in the maintenance of equilibrium in the various sectors of the economy. This gives rise to a large number of objectives of economic policy the achievement of which depends on a variety of instruments of control and on a number of Government agencies such as the National Economic Development Council with its regional bodies, the Regional Development Councils and the Monopolies Commission. These agencies are often policy-forming bodies whose activities have side effects on the economy which it is not always easy to disentangle. Economic management of the economy requires that the various policies are co-ordinated and subordinated to the overriding objectives of stability and growth. To this end a steady flow of information is essential. There must also be a system of analysing the facts speedily so that wise decisions can be made. Computable models of the economy assist in the understanding of the effects of alternative policies. These models can be updated and the overall effects of different controls may be assessed by means of electronic computers. Each model is a set of mathematical relationships describing economic development and is useful as an aid to understanding how the economy works. The estimates of public expenditure for future years published in the Government's White

Paper may be combined with various hypothetical balance-of-payments positions and assumptions about consumer expenditure. Various rates of growth may be applied to these figures and the results analysed by computer. An economic model may be subdivided into its component parts in the form of expenditure categories of goods and services such as motor vehicles, fuel and oil, electrical goods, etc. Various categories of expenditure in the public sector may be distinguished, e.g. defence, education, roads and public lighting. From these categories probable future demands on individual industries may be ascertained. The preparation of sub-models allows for rapid updating in the event of the discovery of new production processes or changes in products as a result of new inventions, etc. Thus the computer and economic models using reliable data may assist the Government to choose appropriate economic policies in order to attain its various objectives.

FUNCTIONS OF PUBLIC EXPENDITURE

One of the driving forces behind the growth of public expenditure is the rising standard of living in the country as a whole. When real incomes are rising public expenditure is less concerned with the relief of poverty than with the provision of motorways, new towns, new colleges and hospitals and the development of the theatre, music and the visual arts. As people become better off, the social environment needs to be improved in order to keep the balance. This is one of the functions of the public sector of the economy, since the private sector tends to leave out of account the non-economic advantages of activity. It is possible to divide the functions of the public sector into three kinds. The first of these comprises measures to exercise a general regulation of the economy in the interests of stability and growth. The second consists of entering production directly by providing social services or by providing goods and services through public corporations which are in control of nationalized industries. The third involves the Government in measures designed to control specific sectors of the economy and includes policies concerned with monopolies, with agriculture, with housing, with shipbuilding, etc. These public-sector functions are performed within the legal and institutional framework of the economy. The banking system, financial institutions such as the Stock Exchange and the law relating to contracts, for example, may be taken as given; although from time to time changes occur in this framework also. In any case the institutional arrangements in one country may differ from those in another and, just as private business firms cross national boundaries, so may public corporations and private companies. The growth of large international companies dealing in such things as motor vehicles, oil, tobacco, frozen foods, washing powders, etc., has resulted in these companies taking the world as their market so that production takes place in a number of different countries. Government economic policy impinges on these international companies just as it does on domestic firms, but much of the profit made by the former remains to finance future operations as well as accruing to the Government in taxation. A country benefits, not only from the investment of capital in plant and machinery brought by international business, but also by the technical knowledge and management skills which are disseminated. The benefits show themselves in additional employment and in an increased rate of growth of national income.

The economic situation changes from month to month and Government policy must take account of these short-term changes as well as look ahead to the long-term problems. Fiscal and monetary policies form the foundations of the Government's management of the economy but within these broad policies there is a wide choice of instruments. There are various ways of restricting credit. There are many different taxes which may be altered. New taxes may be introduced. By what criteria can the success or failure of Government economic policy be judged? The question can only be properly answered if the objectives of policy are themselves known. If one of the aims is to secure a rate of growth of national output of 4 per cent per annum and another is to reduce the rate of inflation to $\frac{1}{2}$ per cent per annum it is possible that relative success in one direction may mean relative failure in another since a growth rate of, say, 3·5 per cent may be achieved only at the expense of an inflation of prices greater than $\frac{1}{2}$ per cent. The maintenance of full employment may be translated into a figure of, say, 3 per cent of unemployed manpower but this objective may not be reached if price stability is regarded as an essential goal. Thus, there may be a conflict of objectives in the sense that not all are attainable at the same time. Government policy must therefore decide on priorities and take into account a certain amount of deviation on either side of a given objective. For each objective, the outturn may be compared with the forecast, and the probable cause of discrepancy investigated. This process may be applied to such aggregates as G.N.P., consumption, public investment, private investment, productivity and the balance of payments.

Government decisions on economic policy are inevitably decisions about the allocation of resources. The economic objectives of society involve the problem of choice and allocation. This choice takes place in a dynamic economy in which flexibility and adaptation are required. The private sector of the economy, since it is based on profitability, is constantly creating new spheres of activity, new occupations and new methods. Successful business firms are generally the efficient ones, which make the best possible use of available resources, even if this means that they must move from one industry into another. In the public sector, changes are usually less spectacular, but flexibility of attitude and willingness to introduce new procedures and processes lead to greater efficiency. The greater the quantity of resources utilized by the public sector the less is available in the private sector. The greater the amount of resources allocated to investment in conditions of full employment, the less will be available for immediate consumption. The redistribution of the command over resources through taxation and expenditure on social security, if carried too far, may react on the quantity of resources available in the future. Government economic policy, whether fiscal, monetary or consisting of direct controls, is concerned, in the final analysis, with the allocation of resources in order to satisfy the economic wants of the community.

QUESTIONS ON CHAPTER 12

1. Why should the Government interfere with the free working of the price system in the case of housing?

2. "In order to relieve pressure on the educational and health services more people should be encouraged to pay out of their own pockets." Discuss.

3. What do you consider to be the major economic problems currently facing the Government and what steps are being taken to deal with these problems?

4. What is the significance of cost–benefit analysis in appraising the efficiency of Government activity?

5. For what reasons might the Government wish to control monopolistic practices and how might this be accomplished?

6. Since steady increases in wages and salaries are generally desired, why does the Government often view them disapprovingly?

7. "Government expenditure on current goods and services should be paid for out of taxation; capital investment should be financed by borrowing." Discuss.

8. Read the following passage carefully and write out your comments.

INFLATION WITH UNEMPLOYMENT

Many of the ideas about balancing the economy along a path of steady growth between under-employment on the one hand, and inflation on the other, are based on the theories of Keynes which find expression in his *General Theory of Employment, Interest and Money*. These ideas reflect the underlying assumptions that national output and aggregate employment vary directly with each other and that employment and national income also vary together in the same direction. This means that when output increases, so does employment; and when income increases, employment does also. Under a set of relationships such as these, under-employment and inflation are opposite sides of the same coin. The proper policy to follow is one which expands or contracts aggregate spending in the economy.

Suppose, however, that the relationships are not quite like this. Suppose that there is no direct relationship between employment of labour and output. This could happen if the economy were nearing a state of automation where machines were being controlled by computers rather than by manpower. In this case additional output would mean the additional employment of capital equipment and automated machinery instead of the use of additional manpower. Suppose, also, that the relationship between income and employment was upset. This could easily happen in a community where social security had been carried so far that unemployed labour received a benefit equal to the wage foregone. Increasing unemployment would not then result in a diminishing national money income but, on the contrary, spending could be maintained (and even increased somewhat out of savings).

Under such circumstances might not the phenomenon of inflation with unemployment emerge?

What is the remedy for this state of affairs? On the face of it the answer is as follows:

(i) reduce the length of the working day as output becomes more and more automated;

(ii) introduce an incomes policy to maintain incomes within the annual increase in productivity;

(iii) prevent social security benefits from rising as fast as income.

Unfortunately many pressures are at work in the economy to make these measures unpopular and even politically inexpedient. Hence the continued interest shown by both economists and politicians in the use of monetary policy as a curb to inflation by affecting total spending. "Real" factors such as unemployment of manpower and changes in output are not as amenable to monetary controls, however, as are the volume of saving, credit or total money supply and interest rates.

References and Further Reading

National Income

National Income and Expenditure, current edition (H.M.S.O.)
EDEY, H. C., & PEACOCK, A. T., *National Income and Social Accounting* (Hutchinson)

The Private Sector

CAIRNCROSS, A. K., *An Introduction to Economics* (Butterworth)
DORFMAN, R., *Prices and Markets* (Prentice-Hall)
PAISH, F. W., *Benham's Economics* (Pitman)

The Public Sector

HICKS, U. K., *Public Finance* (Nisbet)
HOUGHTON, R. W., ed., *Public Finance* (Penguin)
MUSGRAVE, R. A., *Theory of Public Finance* (McGraw-Hill)
PEACOCK, A. T. & WISEMAN, J., *The Growth of Public Expenditure in the United Kingdom* (Allen & Unwin)
PREST, A. R., *Public Finance in Theory and Practice* (Weidenfeld & Nicolson)
SANDFORD, C. T., *Economics of Public Finance* (Pergamon)
WILLIAMS, A., *Public Finance and Budgetary Policy* (Allen & Unwin)

The Banking Sector

HARROD, R. F., *Money* (Macmillan)
HOCKLEY, G. C., *Monetary Policy and Public Finance* (Routledge)
Report of Committee on Working of the Monetary System, Cmd. 827 (H.M.S.O.)

Current Literature

Preliminary Estimates of National Income and Balance of Payments (H.M.S.O.)

REFERENCES AND FURTHER READING

Bank of England Quarterly Bulletin
Annual White Paper on Public Expenditure (H.M.S.O.)
Economic Trends, monthly (H.M.S.O.)
Financial Statistics, monthly (H.M.S.O.)
Financial Statement and Budget Report (H.M.S.O.)
and the various bank reviews, e.g. *The National–Westminster Quarterly Bulletin*

Index

157